Soy City Foods

Vegetarian Cookbook

ACKNOWLEDGEMENTS: Our thanks to all the chefs at the Vegetarian Restaurants and special friends of Soy City Foods who provided us with their favourite recipes.

Front Cover Photo: From top right, clockwise: Tempeh Macaroni Salad, Quick Stuffed Mushrooms, Pecan Crusted Tempeh, Harvest Dinner Reuben, Quick Tempeh Pizza. See Rapid Recipes for instructions.

Back Cover Photo: From top right, clockwise: Tofu Cheesecake, Black Bottom Pie, Maple Pecan Bars, Soymash Macaroons, Banana Date Chews, Banana Soymash Muffins. See Desserts for instructions.

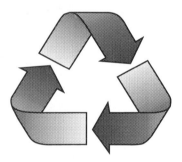

This book is printed on recycled paper.

Printed in Canada

Soy City Foods

Vegetarian Cookbook

Proven recipes from the kitchens of
The Vegetarian Restaurants

Toronto, Canada, 1991

Introduction

The contributions of the vegetarian and organic foods movements to nutrition and the art of cookery are just beginning to be felt in the larger community.

Until recently, manufacturers of health and vegetarian foods have often compromised on nutrition in order to gain a more favourable position in the market. They have produced meat look-alike and taste-alike substitutes, by torturing the various fats and proteins into a semblance of meat, which they felt the public palate demanded.

Soy City Foods has resisted this trend by producing a unique series of whole-bean and soymash products which are high in nutritional value. As people have become more aware of the need for healthy, nutritious food and have begun to value food quality over mere looks and taste, they are now willing to select foods which have their own unique, though perhaps unfamiliar, tastes. Products made from soybeans are typical of these new foods and very often, although the "bite" and taste may not be the usual, they are judged delicious.

Some History

In 1975, The Golden Age Food Limited. opened the Vegetarian Restaurant in downtown Toronto. We hoped to supply a source of healthy vegetarian foods for a local community which was health conscious. We produced many delicious dishes there, but we were hampered by a lack of healthy soy-based products from organically grown soybeans, with which we could quickly prepare nutritious meals. We solved this problem by creating our own production facility. Soy City Foods provided us with some basic products which we developed and perfected over the years.

This Book

These products are now available nation-wide and, to complement them, we have gathered here our best recipes which have been created and tested in our own restaurants. You will find them to be excellent tasting and nutritious and you can be assured that you are offering your family dishes which will help you all maintain a healthy lifestyle.

We sincerely hope you try many of the dishes. If you have difficulty obtaining any of our products, please contact us and we will provide you with the name of our nearest distributor.

Soy City Foods
2847 Dundas Street West
Toronto, Ontario.
M6P 1Y6

Telephone (416) 762-1257
Fax (416) 767-4112

Table of Contents

Dips, Spreads, & Sauces

Makes 3 Cups

Tofu Avocado Dip

Ingredients

250 g	Tofu
2	Ripe Avocados
3 Tbsp.	Olive Oil
2 Tbsp.	Cider Vinegar
1 tsp.	Lemon Juice
1 tsp.	Tamari
2 Cloves	Garlic, Minced
1 Small	Onion, Chopped
	Chili Powder

Directions

Blend all ingredients, except chili powder, in blender or food processor until smooth.

Add more tamari or sea salt, if desired.

Sprinkle with chili powder.

Makes 1 Cup

GARLIC TOFU DIP

INGREDIENTS

1 Tbsp.	Chopped Chives
2 Cloves	Garlic, Minced
165 g	Tofu
1 Tbsp.	Sunflower Oil
¼ tsp.	Tamari
1 Tbsp.	Water

DIRECTIONS

Chop chives and mince garlic.

Place all ingredients in blender.

Blend until smooth.

Optional:
Omit garlic and add ¼ - ½ teaspoon each of curry powder and ground cumin.

Serves 6

TEMPATÉ

Your guests and family will think you have visited a German deli for this spread

INGREDIENTS

250 g	Grain Tempeh
1 Cup	Nuts: Almonds, Cashews, Sunflower Seeds, etc. or any Combination of These.
1	Egg, Slightly Beaten
1 Medium	Onion, Chopped
¼ Cup	Catsup
1 Tbsp.	Tamari
¼ tsp.	Sea Salt
1 tsp.	Garlic Powder
1 tsp.	Poultry Seasoning
1 Tbsp.	Oil

DIRECTIONS

Steam or boil the tempeh and grate coarsely.

Grind the nuts fine in coffee grinder or blender.

Combine all ingredients and turn into lightly oiled loaf pan.

Bake at 350 degrees F for 45-60 minutes.

May be served with your favourite rye bread or crackers.

This paté is good hot or cold.

Makes 3½ Cups

TOFU SANDWICH SPREAD

INGREDIENTS

165 g	Tofu
2 Tbsp.	Nutritional Yeast
1 Tbsp.	Tamari
½ tsp.	Dry Mustard
1 Tbsp.	Minced Fresh Parsley
2 Tbsp.	Chopped Scallions
1 Tbsp.	Prepared Horseradish
1 tsp.	Lemon Juice
2 Tbsp.	Minced Fresh Dill
5 Tbsp.	Soy or Regular Mayonnaise
To Taste	Sea Salt

DIRECTIONS

Drain tofu and press out excess liquid into towel.

Mash with a fork.

Mix all ingredients together and blend in a blender or food processor.

Serve on toast and sprinkle with cayenne pepper.

Can be used as a spread for any sandwich.

Makes 3 Cups

CHICK PEA TOFU SPREAD

This spread may be used for sandwiches and canapés or for stuffing cherry tomatoes and cucumber boats

INGREDIENTS

½ Small	Onion
½ Stalk	Celery
½ Large	Green Pepper
1 Clove	Garlic
1 Cup	Chick Peas
250 g	Tofu, Crumbled
2 Tbsp.	Water
1 Tbsp.	Tamari
1 tsp.	Lemon Juice
To Taste	Mayonnaise

DIRECTIONS

Finely chop onions, celery and green pepper.

Mince garlic.

Mash chick peas and tofu together.

Blend all ingredients. Chill.

Makes 2 cups

TEMPEH OLIVE SPREAD

A rich spread that delights all those who love olives

INGREDIENTS

125 g	Grain Tempeh
1 8-oz. Can	Pitted Black Olives
3 Tbsp.	Mayonnaise
To Taste	Tamari or
	Sea Salt

DIRECTIONS

Steam or boil tempeh for 10 minutes. Drain.

Finely grate the tempeh.

Slice or mince olives.

Mix all ingredients (omit the salt or tamari if using green olives).

Serve on crackers or as sandwich spread.

Alternative:

Try this recipe using green olives.

Makes 1¼ cups

TOFU WHIPPED CREAM

INGREDIENTS

250 g	Tofu
¼ Cup	Light Oil
¼ Cup	Raw Sugar or
3 Tbsp	Honey
1 tsp.	Vanilla
⅛ tsp.	Sea Salt
1 tsp.	Fresh Lemon Juice
2 Tbsp.	Soy Milk or Water

DIRECTIONS

Blend all ingredients in blender or food processor until smooth and creamy.

Chill.

Whip with a spoon just before serving.

Makes 2 cups

TOFU THOUSAND ISLAND DRESSING

INGREDIENTS

125 g	Tofu
1 Cup	Soy Mayonnaise
¼ Cup	Catsup
	Juice of ½ Lemon
½ tsp.	Sea Salt
1½ tsp.	Prepared Horseradish
¼ Cup	Pickle Relish

DIRECTIONS

Blend the first 5 ingredients in a food processor or blender until smooth.

Put the blended ingredients in a bowl and add the horseradish and pickle relish. Stir by hand.

Serve over your favourite tossed salad or use as a sauce over the Vegetarian Tofu Burgers.

Makes 1½ cups

TOFU COTTAGE CHEESE

INGREDIENTS

500 g	*Tofu*
¼ tsp.	*Garlic Powder*
1 Tbsp.	*Oriental Sesame Oil*
½ tsp.	*Tamari*
2 Tbsp.	*Lemon Juice*

DIRECTIONS

Steam the tofu for 5 minutes and let it cool.

Mix all ingredients together and pulse in a food processor (should have cottage cheese texture).

Serve over salads or vegetables.

Makes 2 cups

CURRY SAUCE

INGREDIENTS

3 Tbsp.	Butter or Light Oil
3 Tbsp.	Unbleached Flour
2 Cups	Soy Milk, Heated
3 Tbsp.	Curry Powder
1 Tbsp.	Coriander
½ tsp.	Cinnamon
1 tsp.	Cumin
1 tsp.	Turmeric
⅛ tsp.	Ground Cloves
1 Tbsp.	Garlic Powder
1 tsp.	Sea Salt
2 tsp.	Prepared Mustard

DIRECTIONS

Melt butter or oil on low heat in a heavy saucepan.

Add flour and stir one minute on medium heat. Cool a few minutes.

Heat soy milk in a separate pan. Heat only to steaming point. Do not boil as soy milk may curdle.

Slowly add the heated soy milk to the flour mixture, stirring constantly.

Add the seasonings and mustard. Continue heating and stirring until thickened. Again, be careful not to boil.

Use with steamed tofu or tempeh and vegetables over rice, or with any dish that needs a curry sauce.

Makes 2 cups

QUICK DIJON SAUCE

INGREDIENTS

1½ Cups	Soy Milk
3 Tbsp.	Butter or Light Oil
3 Tbsp.	Unbleached Flour
1 tsp.	Sea Salt
1 Tbsp.	Lemon Juice
1 10-oz. Jar	Dijon Mustard

DIRECTIONS

Heat soy milk, being careful not to boil.

In a separate heavy saucepan, melt butter on low heat.

Add the flour and stir one minute.

Slowly add the hot milk, stirring constantly.

Add salt, lemon juice and mustard while continuing to stir.

Heat and stir until thickened.

Makes 3½ cups

TOFU DILL SAUCE

INGREDIENTS

4	*Scallions, Chopped*
1 Cup	*Minced Fresh Dill*
2 Cups	*Vegetable Broth*
1 Clove	*Garlic, Minced*
250 g	*Tofu*
To Taste	*Tamari*

DIRECTIONS

Bring vegetable broth, scallions, dill and garlic to a boil.

Simmer 10 minutes. Cool.

Put mixture and tofu in blender. Add tamari and blend until smooth.

Pour over your favourite vegetable. Good especially over fresh asparagus or green beans.

Soups & Salads

MOTHER'S UKRAINIAN BORSCH

For a more satisfying soup we've added tofu

INGREDIENTS

14 Cups	Water
¼ Small	Cabbage, Chopped
½ Cup	Chopped Parsley
1¼ Cup	Peeled, Cubed Beets
1¼ Cups	Cubed Potatoes
1½ Stalks	Celery, Sliced
1½ Cups	Cubed Carrots
2 Cups	Chopped Onion
3 Tbsp.	Sunflower Oil
500 g	Frozen Tofu, Thawed
¼ Cup	Tamari
¼ Cup	Water
1 Tbsp.	Basil
2 Tbsp.	Dill Weed
1	Bay Leaf
Pinch	Thyme
6 - 8 Cloves	Garlic, Pressed
2 Tbsp.	Tomato Paste

DIRECTIONS

Bring water to a boil in a 6 quart stock pot. Add cabbage, parsley, beets, potatoes, celery, and carrots. Return to a boil and simmer for 30 minutes.

Meanwhile, sauté onion with oil in an iron skillet until nicely browned. Remove onion from the pan and set aside. Keep oiled skillet for the next step.

Squeeze the excess water from the thawed tofu and cut it into ¾-inch cubes.

Combine water and tamari and toss with the tofu. Drain excess liquid and sauté the tofu for several minutes.

Check the cooking vegetables and when the potatoes are tender, add the herbs, sautéed onions, and garlic. Simmer for 10 minutes more and then add sautéed tofu and tomato paste.

Cook for 5 minutes. Remove bay leaf before serving.

Serve hot.

Serves 8-10

CORN CHOWDER SUPREME

Serves 5

INGREDIENTS

1 Large	Onion, Chopped
1 Large Stalk	Celery, Chopped
1 Medium	Green Pepper, Chopped
3 Medium	Potatoes, Cubed
1½ Tbsp.	Oil
	or
½ Cup	Water
4 Cups	Corn
2 tsp.	Sea Salt
½ tsp.	Thyme
½ tsp.	Marjoram
½ tsp.	Oregano
250 g	Tofu
1 Cup	Cashews, Ground

DIRECTIONS

Sauté first 4 ingredients in oil or water for about 10 minutes.

Add corn, seasonings and enough water to completely cover vegetables.

Bring to a boil, reduce heat, simmer until potatoes are tender.

Place tofu in blender with some of the soup broth and blend until smooth.

Add tofu mixture to the vegetables.

Finely grind cashews in a coffee grinder or blender and add to the soup as a thickener.

Adjust seasonings.

Serve immediately.

Serves 2-3

TOFU NOODLE SOUP

This recipe is just as comforting as Mama's chicken noodle

INGREDIENTS

5 Cups	Water
2 Cups	Egg Noodles
250 g	Tofu
⅓ Cup	Engevita Yeast
1 Tbsp.	Basil
1 Tbsp.	Garlic Powder
To Taste	Sea Salt
2 Tbsp.	Unsalted Butter or Olive Oil

DIRECTIONS

Boil the water and add the egg noodles.

Dice the tofu small and add to water.

Add the yeast and seasonings.

Simmer until noodles are cooked.

Add salt to taste.

Add the butter or olive oil just before serving.

SWEET POTATO TAHINI SOUP

Serves 6

Just the right soup after a morning of raking leaves

INGREDIENTS

5 Cups	Water
2 Medium	Carrots, Diced
2 Large	Yams, Diced
1 Large	Potato, Diced
1 Large	Onion, Diced
2 tsp.	Garlic Powder
1 Tbsp.	Basil
To Taste	Sea Salt
⅓ Cup	Tahini
⅓ Cup	Engivita Yeast
250 g	Tofu, Cubed
Optional:	
2 Tbsp.	Butter

DIRECTIONS

Boil the water and add carrots, yams, potato, onion, garlic powder, basil, and sea salt.

Simmer until vegetables are tender.

Blend in a blender half of the soup mix, adding tahini, butter, if desired, yeast, and tofu.

Return to saucepan and reheat before serving.

Serves 6-8

KOREAN TOFU SOUP

INGREDIENTS

3 Sheets	Nori
1 Cup	Water, Lukewarm
6 Cups	Vegetable Stock or Vegetable Bouillon
1 Medium	Onion, Chopped
2 Cloves	Garlic, Minced
½ Cup	Sliced Celery
1 Cup	Sliced Mushrooms
500 g	Tofu
1 Tbsp.	Miso
1 Tbsp.	Oriental Sesame Oil
3 Tbsp.	Chopped Parsley
2 tsp.	Fresh Grated Ginger
To Taste	Tamari

DIRECTIONS

Soak nori in water for 1 hour; then cook 15 minutes. Drain.

Heat stock, adding nori.

Meanwhile, sauté onions, garlic, celery, and mushrooms in oil until almost tender.

Cut tofu into ½-inch cubes.

Dissolve miso in 3 Tbsp. water and add to stock.

Add vegetables, tofu and all remaining ingredients to stock. Bring to boil, reduce heat, simmer for 15 minutes.

Serves 8-12

INDIAN MULLIGATAWNY SOUP FOR A CROWD

INGREDIENTS

2 Cups	Cooked Chick Peas
1 Tbsp.	Oil
2 Tbsp.	Butter
¾ Cup	Onion, Minced
¾ Cup	Chopped Carrot
¾ Cup	Chopped Celery
½ Cup	Chopped Turnip
⅔ Cup	Chopped Green Pepper
¾ Cup	Chopped Apple (optional)
2 tsp.	Sea Salt
½ tsp.	Cayenne Pepper
1½ tsp.	Curry powder
6 Cups	Vegetable Stock
1 Tbsp.	Cornstarch
¼ Cup	Cold Water
¼ Cup	Tomato Paste
500 g	Tofu, Cubed
	Fresh Parsley, Chopped

DIRECTIONS

Purée the chick peas.

Heat oil and butter in pot. Add onion, carrot, celery, and turnip and sauté 5 minutes. Add green pepper, apple, and seasonings, and sauté for 5 minutes. Set aside.

Heat vegetable stock to boiling. Make a paste of the cornstarch and water and add to stock, stirring constantly until it comes to a boil.

Add vegetable mixture, chick pea purée, tomato paste, and tofu to stock. Simmer, until vegetables are tender. Garnish with fresh chopped parsley.

Serves 4-6

CHINESE TOFU SOUP

INGREDIENTS

6	*Dried Chinese Straw Mushrooms*
6 Cups	*Water*
4	*Vegetable Bouillon Cubes*
1 Cup	*Bamboo Shoots, Sliced - Reserve Liquid from the Can*
½ Cup	*Chopped Celery*
¼ Head	*Savoy Cabbage, Chopped*
375 g	*Tofu, Finely Diced*
5 Tbsp.	*Tamari*
Optional:	
6 Drops	*Oriental Sesame Oil*
3	*Scallions, Chopped*

DIRECTIONS

Soak Chinese mushrooms in water for 15 minutes. Discard the water, then dice.

In a large pot, combine the 6 Cups water, bouillon cubes, and juice from the bamboo shoots. Bring to a boil and add celery, bamboo shoots, mushrooms, and cabbage. Boil for 1 minute.

Add tofu, tamari, and sesame oil. Simmer 4-5 minutes.

Garnish with scallions.

Serve immediately.

INDONESIAN MARINATED TEMPEH SALAD

A Soy City Foods staff favourite

Serves 5-6

INGREDIENTS

500 g	Grain Tempeh
¼ Cup	Sesame Seeds
½ Cup	Cashews
2	Scallions, Chopped
l Large	Green Pepper, Chopped
1 Stalk	Celery, Sliced Diagonally
Optional:	
	Fresh Bean Sprouts
	Fresh Parsley
	Toasted Coconut

Dressing:

¾ Cup	Orange Juice
½ Cup	Sunflower Oil
1 Tbsp.	Oriental Sesame Oil
2 Tbsp.	Tamari
	Juice of 1 Lemon
1-2 Cloves	Garlic, Minced
½ tsp.	Grated Fresh Ginger or
¼ tsp.	Powdered Ginger

DIRECTIONS

Steam or boil the grain tempeh for 10 minutes.

Drain.

Roast the sesame seeds and cashews in a dry frying pan, being careful not to burn them.

Put all salad ingredients into a large bowl.

Mix all dressing ingredients together before pouring over the salad.

Serve cold or at room temperature.

May be served with noodles.

Makes 4½ cups

Eggless Tofu Salad

A good alternative if you are trying to cut down on cholesterol

Ingredients

500 g	Tofu, Crumbled
½ Cup	Finely Chopped Red and/or Green Peppers
½ Cup	Chopped Scallions
½ Cup	Finely Chopped Parsley
2 Tbsp.	Chopped Fresh Dill
2½ tsp.	Dijon Mustard
2 Tbsp.	Tamari
2 Tbsp.	Lemon Juice
½ tsp.	Turmeric
1 tsp.	Garlic Powder
1 tsp.	Chili Powder
½ Cup	Mayonnaise or Soy Mayonnaise
To Taste	Sea Salt

Directions

In a medium-sized bowl, combine the crumbled tofu, the vegetables, chopped parsley and dill.

In a separate bowl, combine the remaining ingredients. Add this to the tofu-vegetable mixture and stir thoroughly.

Serve on your favourite bread or rolls.

May be served on crackers as a canapé.

KOREAN VEGETABLE TOFU SALAD

Serves 4-6

INGREDIENTS

500 g	Firm Tofu
1 Medium	Carrot, Julienned
1 Small	Zucchini, Julienned
1 Stalk	Celery, Julienned
1 Medium	Red Sweet Pepper, Sliced
1 Medium	Green Pepper, Sliced
1 Small Can	Baby Ears of Corn
1 Can	Water Chestnuts
1 Cup	Mung Bean Sprouts
2 Tbsp.	Minced Fresh Parsley

Dressing:

1 Cup	Sunflower Oil
¼ Cup	Peanut Butter
¼ Cup	Lemon Juice
1½ Tbsp.	Chili Powder
2 Cloves	Garlic, Crushed
2 Tbsp.	Chopped Onion
2 Tbsp.	Tamari
1 tsp.	Grated Fresh Ginger,

DIRECTIONS

Drain all canned vegetables. Place all of the vegetables in a large bowl.

Cube the tofu and add to the vegetables.

Whisk together the dressing ingredients, or blend in a blender.

Add the dressing to salad and refrigerate, allowing the tofu and vegetables to marinate .

Can be used as a cold entrée when served over noodles of your choice.

Optional:

Prepare a second batch of dressing to serve on the side.

Serves 8-10

TOFUNA SALAD

INGREDIENTS

1 19-oz. Can	Chick Peas
⅓ Cup	Tahini
1 Tbsp.	Tamari
½ tsp.	Garlic Powder
1,250 g	Crumbled Tofu
1 Bunch	Scallions, Finely Chopped
⅓ - ½ Cup	Mayonnaise
1 tsp.	Lemon Juice
Optional:	
Pinch	Cayenne

DIRECTIONS

In a blender or food processor mix chick peas (including liquid), tahini, tamari and garlic powder.

After blending, turn into a bowl and add other ingredients. Mix well.

Side Dishes

Serves 6

TEMPEH SUSHI

INGREDIENTS

1 lb.	*Short Grain Brown Rice*
500 g	*Grain Tempeh*
1 Cup	*Pickle Juice or Herbed Vinegar*
½ Cup	*Prepared Horseradish*
1½ Cups	*Tamari*
2 Medium	*Beets*
2 Large	*Carrots*
1 Bunch	*Scallions*
12-24 Sheets	*Nori*

DIRECTIONS

Prepare rice as usual but stir once or twice to make sticky. Boil or steam the tempeh for 15 minutes. Pour pickle juice over the rice and refrigerate until ready to use.

Combine the horseradish and tamari and put into large baking dish for marinating.

Slice cooked tempeh into 12 lengths and marinate in the tamari-horseradish marinade. Refrigerate until ready to use.

Slice carrots and beets into matchstick shape and size. Cut green ends of scallions into individual leaves. Cut the white ends into halves lengthwise.

You may choose to roll your sushi with single or double sheets of nori. Place the sheets of nori on a clean dry surface. Starting 1 inch from the bottom, spread rice in a 2-inch wide strip across the width.

Put marinated tempeh in the middle of the rice. Put a few strips of scallions above, a few strips of beets below and a few strips of carrots on top of the tempeh. Sprinkle on a little rice to cover vegetables.

Carefully roll the sheets into a tube shape making roll tight as possible without breaking the nori. Wet fingers in marinade and seal the end of the sheets. Put in a stack until all are rolled. In 15 to 30 minutes rolls will feel moist on the outside and are ready to cut.

With a sharp knife, cut off loose ends. Slice tubes in 1-inch thicknesses. Arrange pieces in floral pattern on a plattter with remaining marinade as a dip.

TEMPEH RICE PILAF

Serves 4-6

INGREDIENTS

250 g	Grain Tempeh
½ Cup	Tamari
½ Cup	Water
1 Cup	Uncooked Brown Rice
2 Tbsp.	Vegetable Oil
½ Cup	Slivered Almonds
1 Cups	Peas
½ Cup	Finely Chopped Carrots
½ Cup	Finely Chopped Celery
2½ Cups	Vegetable Broth
To Taste	Tamari

DIRECTIONS

Boil or steam tempeh for 10 minutes. Drain. Marinate in tamari and water for 10 minutes.

In a heavy skillet, toast the rice on medium heat, stirring constantly.

When the rice is golden brown, place in an oiled casserole dish.

Brown the tempeh in a heavy skillet.

Mix almonds, tempeh, peas, carrots, celery, and tamari to taste, and add to casserole

Pour in vegetable broth.

Cover and bake at 325 degrees F for 1 hour and 30 minutes.

Serves 6

HARVEST DINNER POTATO PATTIES

INGREDIENTS

3	*Harvest Dinner Patties*
5 - 6 Medium	*Potatoes*
	Soy or Dairy Milk
1 tsp.	*Basil*
½ Cup	*Chopped Scallions*
To Taste	*Sea Salt*
	Sunflower Seeds

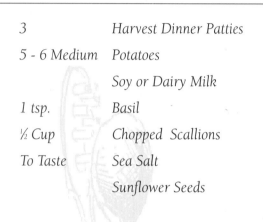

DIRECTIONS

Thaw and bake the Harvest Dinner Patties for 10 minutes at 350 degrees F.

Cut potatoes into cubes and boil or steam. When the potatoes are tender, mash the potatoes with soy or dairy milk. Add basil, chopped scallions, and salt to taste.

Mix the Harvest Dinner Patties with the potatoes.

Form into balls and place onto an oiled cookie sheet. Flatten into patties with a spatula and sprinkle sunflower seeds on top of each patty.

Bake at 400 degrees F for 30 minutes. Serve hot with your favourite mushroom gravy.

Optional:

Use this recipe as a stuffing for green peppers or mushrooms.

Serves 4

KIDS' FAVOURITE FRIES

These are tasty alternatives to the deep fried originals

INGREDIENTS

750 g	Tofu
To Taste	Sea Salt
	Catsup

DIRECTIONS

Preheat oven to 375-400 degrees F.

Slice tofu into long ¼-inch thick shoestrings.

Place on a lightly oiled cookie sheet.

Bake 15 minutes. Turn and bake another 15 minutes or until golden brown.

Serve with sea salt and catsup.

Serves 4

TEMPEH STUFFED BAKED POTATOES

INGREDIENTS

4	*Potatoes*
125 g	*Grain Tempeh*
6	*Mushrooms, Chopped*
1 Medium	*Onion, Chopped*
2 Stalks	*Celery*
2 oz.	*Butter*
1	*Tomato, Skinned and Chopped*
To Taste	*Nutritional Yeast*

Optional Topping:

Grated Cheese

Nutritional Yeast

DIRECTIONS

Scrub and dry potatoes, and prick with a fork.

Bake potatoes at 400 degrees F for 1 hour or until tender. Cut a slice from the top of each potato, let cool a little, then scoop out center.

Prepare tempeh as per package instructions; cut into small cubes.

In a small skillet, sauté mushrooms, onion, tempeh and celery in butter until tender. Add tomato.

Combine this mixture with scooped out potato centres and mix well. Season to taste with nutritional yeast.

Stuff mixture back into the potato jackets. Dot with butter and put back in the oven for 15 minutes.

Top with grated cheese or nutritional yeast.

COLD STUFFED TOMATOES

Makes 8

INGREDIENTS

500 g	Tofu
¼ Cup	Chopped Scallions
1 Tbsp.	Chives
1 tsp.	Tarragon
1	Egg, Hard-boiled, Chopped
¼-½ Cup	Mayonnaise
1 Tbsp.	Chopped Parsley
½ tsp.	Thyme
1 Tbsp.	Basil
2 Cloves	Garlic, Minced
1 tsp.	Tamari
8	Tomatoes, Cored
To Taste	Sea Salt

DIRECTIONS

Crumble tofu into a saucepan, cover with water and bring to a boil.

Simmer about 5 minutes or until firm. Cool and drain.

Combine remaining ingredients with tofu. Mix well.

Chill thoroughly.

Core tomatoes and stuff with chilled mixture.

Quick & Easy Recipes

Serves 4-6

HARVEST DINNER TACOS

A fun way to introduce children to a meatless meal

INGREDIENTS

12	*Precooked Taco Shells*
4	*Harvest Dinner Patties*

Possible Toppings:

Chopped Onions

Chopped Tomatoes

Shredded Lettuce

Alfalfa Sprouts

Diced Avocado

Grated Cheese

Hot Salsa

DIRECTIONS

Prepare small bowls of each topping you wish to serve.

Cook the Harvest Dinner Patties on a non-stick skillet (no oil is required) until nice and brown on both sides, or bake in a toaster oven. Break into chunks into a bowl.

Preheat your taco shells while the patties are cooking.

Place all ingredients on the table so that family or friends can choose their fillings buffet style.

Serves 1

HARVEST DINNER REUBEN

A hearty open-faced sandwich with a German flair

INGREDIENTS

1	*Harvest Dinner Patty*
	Your Favourite Rye Bread
	Mayonnaise or Tofu Sandwich Spread
	Sauerkraut, Drained
	Cheese, Soy or Dairy

DIRECTIONS

Cook patty according to the directions on the box.

Spread rye bread with your favourite sandwich spread.

Place patty on the bread and top with sauerkraut and then thinly sliced cheese.

Place under broiler just until cheese melts.

Serve immediately.

Serves 4-5

HEARTY TEMPEH BURGER

All you need here is to whip up a big batch of Kids' Favourite Fries

INGREDIENTS

250 g	Grain Tempeh
2 Tbsp.	Chopped Scallions
2 Tbsp.	Light Oil
½ Cup	Sesame Seeds
¼ Cup	WW Flour
2 Tbsp.	Tahini
2	Eggs, Beaten
2 tsp.	Tamari
½ tsp.	Basil
2 Cloves	Garlic, Minced
½ tsp.	Sea Salt
Optional:	Tomato Salsa or Tartar Sauce

DIRECTIONS

Boil or steam the grain tempeh for 10 minutes. Drain.

Mash tempeh and mix in all other ingredients except salsa or tartar sauce.

Form into balls and flatten into patties.

Place on lightly oiled baking sheet.

Bake at 350 degrees F for 30 minutes.

Optional:

Serve with a tomato salsa or tartar sauce.

Serves 4

OPEN-FACED TEMPEH SANDWICH WITH HORSERADISH BUTTER

This sandwich looks just as good as it tastes

INGREDIENTS

250 g	Grain Tempeh
½ Cup	Tamari
½ Cup	Water
½ Medium	Red Sweet Pepper
1 Stalk	Celery
1 Small	Red Onion
½ Bunch	Parsley
1½ Cups	Sauerkraut, Drained
⅓ Cup	Butter
3 Tbsp.	Prepared Horseradish
4 tsp.	Dijon Mustard
4 Slices	Rye Bread
Optional:	
	Tomato Slices
	Olives

DIRECTIONS

Boil or steam tempeh for 10 minutes. Cut it in half and then slice each half horizontally so that you have four thin rectangles. Marinate tempeh in tamari and water.

Finely chop the pepper, celery, onion, and parsley and combine with the sauerkraut.

Brown the slices of tempeh on a lightly oiled griddle or teflon frying pan. Set aside to cool.

Blend in a food processor the butter, horseradish, and mustard.

Generously spread the butter mixture on the rye bread. Add a few tablespoons of the sauerkraut mix, then 1 slice of tempeh.

Top with a generous portion of sauerkraut mixture.

Garnish the sandwiches with slices of tomato and/or olives.

Serve at room temperature.

Serves 2

TOFU DELIGHT

INGREDIENTS

250 g	Tofu
¼ Cup	Engevita Yeast
To Taste	Tamari
⅓ Cup	Chopped Onions
½ Cup	Sliced Mushrooms
2	WW Pita Bread
	"Tofu Sandwich Spread" or Mayonnaise
	Sliced Tomatoes
	Alfalfa Sprouts

DIRECTIONS

Cut tofu in ½-inch thick slices.

Put the engevita yeast in a bowl and dip the tofu slices into the bowl, allowing the yeast to coat both sides of the tofu.

Put the breaded tofu slices in a lightly oiled frying pan and sprinkle with tamari. Cook over low heat until both sides of the tofu are browned.

Sauté the onions and mushrooms. Put tofu, mushrooms, and onions in a warmed whole wheat pita bread. Add some "Tofu Sandwich Spread" or mayonnaise, sliced tomatoes, and alfalfa sprouts.

Tofu prepared this way may also be combined with steamed vegetables and a whole grain.

Serves 10-12

QUICK STUFFED MUSHROOMS

A tasty appetizer to introduce your friends to soy foods

INGREDIENTS

2 doz. Large	Mushrooms
2 Tbsp.	Lemon Juice
1 tsp.	Minced Fresh Parsley
1 Small	Onion
2 Cloves	Garlic
1 Tbsp.	Olive Oil
1 tsp.	Oregano
2	Harvest Dinner Patties, Thawed
½ Cup	Vegetable Broth or Bouillon
Optional:	
To Taste	Sea Salt
	Cayenne
	Soy or Dairy Cheese

DIRECTIONS

Wash mushrooms. Remove and save stems. Toss mushroom caps in lemon juice.

Chop finely the mushroom stems, parsley and the onion.

Crush the garlic and sauté it along with the onion, the mushroom stems and parsley in olive oil (or steam in small amount of water in the skillet).

Add the oregano and cayenne, if desired, and sea salt.

Crumble the Harvest Dinner Patties as you add them to the above mixture. Sauté a few minutes.

Add just enough vegetable broth for the mixture to hold together.

Stuff mushroom caps with the patty mixture.

Place the mushroom caps in a shallow baking pan. Pour remaining broth around the mushrooms.

Bake at 350 degrees F for 20 minutes.

Remove from oven.

Add cheese, if desired, at this time.

Place under the broiler (with or without cheese) for a few minutes to brown.

Makes 12-16 small patties

TOFU ALMOND PATTIES

INGREDIENTS

2 Cups	Water
1 tsp.	Sea Salt
½ Cup	Brown Rice
⅓ Cup	Almonds
500 g	Tofu
2 Tbsp.	Tamari
2 tsp.	Garlic Powder
2 tsp.	Onion Powder
1 Tbsp.	Dried Parsley
½ Cup	Oat Bran
1 Small	Onion, Chopped

DIRECTIONS

Bring 1 cup salted water to a boil. Add brown rice. Reduce heat and simmer on low for 40 to 50 minutes until all of the water has been absorbed.

Grind almonds in a blender or coffee grinder.

In a blender or food processor, blend half of the tofu, 1 cup cooked rice, 1 cup water, tamari and spices.

Mash the other 250 g of the tofu and mix with any remaining rice. Add the chopped onion, oat bran, almonds, and blended ingredients. Mix well.

Drop by spoonfuls onto a lightly oiled cookie sheet. Flatten to form patties.

Bake at 350 degrees F for 30 minutes.

Note: The mixture can be made ahead and refrigerated.

Serves 2

QUICK TEMPEH DINNER

INGREDIENTS

250 g	Grain Tempeh

Sauce #1 Tamari-Ginger:

6 Tbsp.	Tamari
1⅓ Cup	Water
2 tsp.	Ginger
¼ Cup	Chopped Scallions

Sauce #2 Mushroom-Onion:

1⅓ Cup	Water
4 Tbs.	Tamari
1 Cup	Chopped Onions
1 Cup	Chopped Mushrooms

Sauce #3

Your Own	BBQ Sauce
	Tomato Sauce
	Stewed Tomatoes
	Picante Sauce

DIRECTIONS

Place frozen grain tempeh in an 8-inch square casserole.

Sauce #1 and #2:

Shake all ingredients in a jar.

Pour on sauce of your choice, enough to cover ½ inch over the top of the tempeh. Insure that there is some of the sauce under the tempeh as well.

Bake at 350 degrees F for 1 hour.

CHILI CON TEMPEH

Serves 4

INGREDIENTS

250 g	Grain Tempeh
½ Cup	Tamari
½ Cup	Water
1 Large	Onion
1 Cup	Cooked Kidney Beans
1 Cup	Spaghetti Sauce
2 Tbsp.	Chili Powder

DIRECTIONS

Mince the tempeh and place in a bowl. Cover with a mixture of the water and the tamari. Set aside to marinate.

Chop onion and sauté slowly in 4 Tbsp. of water in a large pan until onion is translucent.

Add kidney beans with their liquid, the spaghetti sauce and the chili powder. Then simmer for ½ hour.

Drain tempeh and add to sauce mixture. Add tamari to taste if necessary. Simmer for an additional ½ hour.

Serves 6

PECAN RICE TOFU PATTIES

INGREDIENTS

1	Onion, Finely Chopped
2 Cloves	Garlic, Pressed
1 Cup	Cooked Long Grain Rice
1 Cup	Finely Chopped Pecans
1 tsp.	Sunflower Oil
3 Tbsp.	Water
1 tsp.	Sea Salt
275 g	Tofu, Crumbled
1 Cup	WW Bread Crumbs
1	Egg, Beaten
¼ tsp.	Sage
¼ tsp.	Cayenne Pepper

DIRECTIONS

Pre-heat oven to 350 degrees F.

Sauté the onions and garlic in oil and water until tender.

Mix all ingredients and form into patties.

Place on lightly oiled baking sheet.

Bake approximately 30 minutes until golden brown.

Serve with your favourite gravy.

Serves 2

QUICK SKILLET CASSEROLE

INGREDIENTS

½ Cup	Water
1 Medium	Onion, Chopped
½ Large	Red Sweet Pepper, Chopped
1 Cup	Cooked Brown Rice
1	Harvest Dinner Patty, Hickory Flavour
1 Cup	Fresh Parsley, Chopped
4	Eggs, Lightly Beaten
1 Tbsp.	Tamari
⅛ tsp.	Basil
⅛ tsp.	Oregano or Marjoram
⅛ tsp.	Thyme

DIRECTIONS

Simmer the chopped onion in a pan with ½ cup water for 3 minutes, then add the chopped pepper and simmer for 2 more minutes.

To the simmering onion and pepper mixture, add the rice, Harvest Dinner Patty (crumbled), parsley, eggs, tamari, and all of the herbs, waiting 1 minute between each addition, and distribute each ingredient evenly over the cooking surface.

Cover the pan and cook for 5 more minutes over medium heat.

Serve with hot buttered pita bread, Tabasco sauce, and a nice green salad.

Serves 2

Harvest Dinner Quiche

Ingredients

1 10-inch	WW Pie Shell
1 Tbsp.	Butter
½ Large	Onion, Chopped
½ Medium	Green Pepper, Chopped
¼ lb.	Fresh Mushrooms, Sliced
1 Large	Tomato, Chopped
½ tsp.	Sea Salt
¼ tsp.	Garlic Powder
½ tsp.	Thyme
1	Harvest Dinner Patty
3	Eggs
1 Cup	Soy or Dairy Milk
1½ Cups	Grated Cheese

Directions

Line a 10-inch pie plate with your favourite whole-wheat pie crust.

Sauté in butter over medium heat the onion, pepper and mushrooms. Add the tomato and seasonings and simmer until tomato is tender. Remove from pan.

Without adding more butter or oil, fry the Harvest Dinner Patty on both sides until well browned.

Beat the eggs with the milk in a medium sized bowl. Add 1 cup of the grated cheese and then the vegetables.

Crumble the Harvest Dinner Patty into this mixture. Pour into pie shell. Top with remaining cheese.

Bake at 350 degrees F for 30 minutes or until knife comes out clean when inserted.

Serves 1

QUICK TEMPEH OR TOFU PIZZA

INGREDIENTS

½ Cup	Cubed Tofu or Grain Tempeh
¼ Cup	Chopped Onion
¼ Cup	Chopped Green Pepper
1 tsp.	Sunflower Oil
1	Pita Bread
½ Cup	Tomato Sauce
4	Slices of Tomato

Optional Toppings:

> Nutritional Yeast
>
> Tamari
>
> Soy or Dairy Cheese, Grated

DIRECTIONS

Preheat oven to 375 degrees F.

If using tempeh, prepare as per package directions.

If using tofu, freeze, thaw and squeeze out water.

Lightly sauté onion, pepper and tempeh or tofu in oil.

Place pita in a pie plate and cover with sauce.

Place the vegetables and tempeh or tofu on top of the sauce, and then add the tomato slices.

Sprinkle with optional topping.

Bake for 15-20 minutes.

Serves 4

TEMPEH MACARONI SALAD

INGREDIENTS

250 g	*Grain Tempeh*
12 oz.	*Macaroni*
1 Cup	*Grated Carrots*
1½ tsp.	*Garlic Powder*
1 19-oz. Can	*Chick Peas, Drained*
To Taste	*Soy or Regular Mayonnaise*
	Tamari

Optional:

Fresh Dill, Chopped

Lemon Juice

DIRECTIONS

Steam the tempeh for 10 minutes. Drain.

Cut the tempeh into ½-inch cubes.

Marinate the tempeh in tamari and, if desired, lemon juice while cooking macaroni.

Cook the macaroni according to directions on the package.

Combine all ingredients and mix well.

Chill if desired, but can be served warm.

For variety, use vegetable rotini instead of macaroni.

HARVEST DINNER
STUFFED ACORN SQUASH

An old favourite made extremely easily and quickly

INGREDIENTS

2	Acorn Squash
3 Tbsp.	Water
4 Tbsp.	Tamari
1 Tbsp.	Honey
2-3	Harvest Dinner Patties Depending on Squash Size

Optional:

Butter

Cayenne

DIRECTIONS

Wash and cut squash into halves. Scrape out the seeds and stringy center.

Place cut side down in a baking pan filled with an inch of water.

Bake in 350 degree F oven until squash is nearly tender.

Meanwhile, place water, tamari, and honey into a sauce pan. Heat over medium heat. Add crumbled Harvest Dinner Patties. Heat and stir until all liquid is absorbed.

Add cayenne pepper.

Remove squash from oven, drain, and turn cut side up.

Make several slices through squash.

If desired place a tsp. of butter in each half.

Fill each half with patty filling and return to oven for 10 to 15 minutes.

Cut each piece of squash in half and serve.

Harvest Dinner
Main Dishes

Please Note: Harvest Dinner Patties (which were 5-oz. patties) are now sold as Soy City Foods' Veggie Burgers (which are 3-oz. patties). Please adjust recipes accordingly.

Serves 6

SHEPHERD'S PIE

INGREDIENTS

1 Large	Onion, Diced
2 Cloves	Garlic, Minced
4 Tbsp.	Butter
1 14-oz. Can	Plum Tomatoes, Chopped
3	Harvest Dinner Patties
1 19-oz. Can	Brown Lentils
1 Tbsp.	Sage
¼ tsp.	Rosemary
¼ tsp.	Thyme
8 Medium	Potatoes
½ Cup	Soy Milk
½ tsp.	Sea Salt
3 Cups	Frozen Peas

DIRECTIONS

Sauté onion and garlic in 1 Tbsp. butter until translucent.

Add drained, chopped tomatoes and sauté 2 minutes.

Crumble and add the Harvest Dinner Patties, the lentils, and herbs. Cook over low heat for 5 minutes.

Quarter potatoes and boil until tender.

Drain water and add remaining butter, soy milk and salt, and mash until fluffy.

Cook peas in ¼ cup water until just thawed.

Butter large casserole and place Harvest Dinner mixture in the bottom.

Drain peas and add to casserole.

Cover with mashed potatoes.

Bake in covered dish for 30 minutes at 350 degrees F. Uncover and bake for an additional 15 minutes.

Serve with gravy.

Prepare Harvest Dinner Gravy Packet just Before Serving.

Serves 4-6

HARVEST DINNER STRATA

This lovely dish is worth the effort for special occasions shared with special people

INGREDIENTS

4 Medium	Potatoes
½ tsp.	Dill Weed
2 Tbsp.	Butter
	Soy or Dairy Milk
To Taste	Sea Salt
2 Medium	Sweet Potatoes
½ tsp.	Coriander
Pinch	Basil
2 Tbsp.	Butter
4	Harvest Dinner Patties
½ Cup	Water
1 Tbsp.	Tamari
2 Medium	Onions, Sliced
Pinch	Basil
1 Clove	Garlic, Minced
1 Cup	Peas
2	Bay Leaves
2 Cups	Corn
½ tsp.	Dill Weed
Optional:	
2 Tbsp.	Butter
	Paprika

DIRECTIONS

Boil the potatoes until tender, drain, and whip with dill weed, butter, salt, and enough milk to make light and fluffy.

Slice sweet potatoes and steam until tender. Mash with coriander, basil, butter, and salt to taste. If potatoes are too dry, add a little of the steaming water.

Place Harvest Dinner Patties onto cookie sheet and bake at 350 degrees F for 20 minutes, until crusted.

Select a 9-inch square casserole dish which will make a nice display of the layers. Press patties into the bottom of the dish.

In water and tamari, sauté the onions, garlic, and basil until the onions are translucent and water almost evaporated.

Add bay leaves to water in bottom of steamer and steam peas until tender. Blend ½ of the cooked peas in a blender or food processor with a little of the steam water. Remove the bay leaf before blending. Add blended mixture to whole peas and set aside. Steam and blend corn in the same manner. Add butter to the blended corn for a creamier texture.

To assemble:

Layer onions on top of patties, followed by sweet potatoes, peas, corn, and mashed potatoes.

Mashed potatoes may be piped in a rosette pattern around the edge for decorative touch.

Dot the potatoes with butter, sprinkle with paprika and bake the casserole at 350 degrees F for 20 minutes.

Photo: Harvest Dinner Strata

Serves 4

STUFFED ZUCCHINI

INGREDIENTS

2 Medium	Zucchini
1 Small	Onion, Minced
2 Cloves	Garlic, Minced
½ lb.	Mushrooms, Minced
2	Harvest Dinner Patties
8 oz.	Tomato Sauce
¼ tsp.	Cayenne
¼ tsp.	Oregano
¼ tsp.	Basil
¼ tsp.	Rosemary
To Taste	Sea Salt
Optional:	
	Oat Bran
	Grated Cheese

DIRECTIONS

Steam the zucchini whole until they start to become tender. Slice in half lengthwise and scoop out the pulp, leaving a sturdy shell. Save the pulp.

Sauté the onion, garlic, mushrooms, and zucchini pulp in small amount of oil or water.

Break Harvest Dinner Patties into small pieces. Add these with tomato sauce and seasonings to the vegetable mixture.

Simmer 15 minutes. Mixture may be too wet depending on size of squash. Add oat bran to compensate.

Fill shells, and top with cheese, if desired.

Return to oven and bake at 350 degrees F until tender 15-20 minutes.

Serves 2

VEGETABLE STROGANOFF WITH CASHEW ALMOND SAUCE

INGREDIENTS

1 Cup	Water
1 tsp.	Vegetable Seasoning
1 Small	Butternut Squash
1	Leek or
1 Medium	Onion
1	Red Sweet Pepper
½ Cup	Raw Cashews
¼ Cup	Raw Almonds
½ Cup	Water
¼ tsp.	Garlic Powder
1 Tbsp.	Tamari
2	Harvest Dinner Patties
	Cooked Brown Rice or Noodles
Garnish:	
	Parsley Sprigs
	Cherry Tomatoes

DIRECTIONS

In a large saucepan, bring 1 cup of water to a boil. Add the vegetable seasoning.

Chop squash into ½-inch cubes. Chop leek, or onion, and pepper.

Add squash to boiling water and cook for approximately 4 minutes. Add leek or onion and boil for 1 more minute. Add the pepper and boil until tender. Set aside.

Grind the nuts as fine as possible. Combine cooked vegetables, ½ cup water, garlic powder and tamari. This will make a thick creamy sauce. Simmer for 5 minutes.

Form Harvest Dinner patties into 1½-inch diameter balls and bake approximately 15 minutes.

Serve these balls over rice or noodles. Ladle the vegetables and sauce over the balls and garnish with parsley and cherry tomatoes.

Serves 6

SOUTHERN STYLE FRITTATA

INGREDIENTS

1	Harvest Dinner Patty
2 Cups	Sliced Yams
2 Cups	Sliced Apples
1 tsp.	Fresh Lemon Juice
¼ tsp.	Cinnamon
⅓ Cup	Demerara Sugar
10	Eggs
2 Tbsp.	Butter, Melted
½ Cup	Chopped Scallions
1¾ Cups	Grated Cheddar Cheese, Soy or Dairy
	Dash of Nutmeg

DIRECTIONS

Bake the Harvest Dinner Patty at 350 degrees F for 20 minutes, then crumble very well.

Steam yams until tender.

Peel and thinly slice apples and then squeeze juice of lemon over them. Toss apples in cinnamon and sugar.

Beat eggs well and add melted butter and scallions. Add crumbled Harvest Dinner Patty.

Layer into well-oiled baking dish as follows:

> ½ yams
> ½ apples coated in sugar and cinnamon
> ½ of the cheese
> remaining yams
> remaining apples

Pour egg mixture over all, making sure it totally covers all ingredients and soaks down to the bottom of the pan (poke holes to aid the process).

Top remaining cheese.

Sprinkle with nutmeg to taste.

Bake for approximately 40 minutes at 350 degrees F.

Serves 4

Italian Harvest Dinner Pie

Ingredients

Shell:

3	*Harvest Dinner Patties*
½ Cup	*Tomato Sauce*
1 Medium	*Onion, Chopped*
1	*Egg*
½ tsp.	*Garlic Powder*

Filling:

2 Medium	*Zucchini, Sliced*
1 Cup	*Shredded Mozzarella Cheese*
½ Cup	*Tomato Sauce*
½ Cup	*Pitted Ripe Olives and/or Sliced Mushrooms*
½ tsp.	*Oregano*
½ tsp.	*Basil*

Directions

To make the crust for the pie, combine the shell ingredients, mix well, and press into the sides and bottom of a 9-inch pie plate. Bake for 15-20 minutes at 400 degrees F.

Combine filling ingredients using only ½ of the cheese.

Place filling into pie shell.

Top with remaining cheese.

Bake at 350 degrees F for 30 minutes.

Serves 6

HARVEST DINNER PINWHEELS

INGREDIENTS

4	Harvest Dinner Patties, Thawed
2	Eggs
½ Cup	Minced Onions
2 Medium	Potatoes, Cubed
1¼ Cup	Frozen Peas
To Taste	Sea Salt
Optional:	
	Butter

Photo: Main Dishes clockwise from top, Tofu Cacciatore, Harvest Dinner Pinwheels, Tofu Manicotti, Tofu and Vegetables in Szechuan Black Bean Sauce.

DIRECTIONS

Sauté minced onions in butter or water or oil until soft and translucent.

Steam potatoes and mash with salt and a bit of butter, if desired. Mix the onions into the potatoes.

Cook the peas, purée and cool.

Mix Harvest Dinner Patties with eggs and pat out on wax paper into a rectangle about ¾-inch thick. Cover one half of the rectangle, along one of the long sides, with a layer of the potatoes. Spread a layer of peas over the other half of the patty rectangle, leaving a 1-inch uncovered margin along the long side.

To Roll:

Starting with the potato-covered long side toward you, lift the wax paper and start rolling the rectangle away from you making a neat roll. Seal the edge. Wrap well with wax paper or plastic wrap.

Chill in freezer for 1½ hours.

Using a sharp serrated knife, cut 2-inch slices off the roll .

Lay cut side down on a lightly oiled baking sheet. Brush with melted butter.

Bake at 350 degrees F for 20 minutes.

HARVEST VEGETABLE PIE

Serves 6-8

INGREDIENTS

1 9-inch	Double Crust Pastry
4	Harvest Dinner Patties
3 Medium	Potatoes
¼ tsp.	Sea Salt
1 Tbsp.	Butter
1½ Cups	Corn
1 Small	Onion
1 Clove	Garlic
1	Red Sweet Pepper
1 Tbsp.	Water, Oil, or Butter
1 Medium	Carrot
1 Medium	Zucchini
1 Tbsp.	Minced Fresh Parsley
1 Tbsp.	Minced Fresh Dill Weed
½ tsp.	Basil
¼ tsp.	Oregano
To Taste	Sea Salt
Optional:	
¾ Cup	Grated Cheese

DIRECTIONS

Prepare your pie crust.

Cut potatoes into sixths and steam. Drain, saving ¼ Cup of the water. Mash the potatoes with ¼ tsp. salt, and butter. Use the drained water to fluff them.

Purée corn.

Crumble Harvest Dinner Patties.

Chop onion and red pepper and crush garlic. Sauté in 1 Tbsp. of water, oil, or butter until tender.

Slice carrot and zucchini. Steam until tender.

Combine sautéed vegetables and steamed vegetables, parsley, dill, basil, oregano, and salt.

Layer the pie in this order: bottom crust, mashed potatoes, Harvest Dinner Patties, puréed corn, cheese (if using), and vegetable mixture. Top with pastry.

Bake at 350 degrees F for 35 minutes or until golden brown.

Serves 6

COLCANNON IN HARVEST DINNER CRUST

INGREDIENTS

3	*Harvest Dinner Patties*
4 Medium	*Potatoes, Cubed*
8 Cups	*Chopped Fresh Kale*
1 Medium	*Onion or*
8	*Scallions, Minced*
2 Cloves	*Garlic, Pressed*
1 Tbsp.	*Butter or Oil*
1	*Red Sweet Pepper, Chopped*
⅓ Cup	*Soy or Dairy Milk*
¼ Cup	*Chopped Parsley*
¾ tsp.	*Sea Salt*

DIRECTIONS

Press thawed Harvest Dinner Patties into bottom and sides of a 2-quart glass baking dish. Bake at 350 degrees F for 10 minutes.

Steam potatoes just until tender. Mash.

Steam kale for one minute or until leaves turn dark green. Drain well.

Sauté onion and garlic in the butter until soft, adding the pepper for the last minute or two.

Combine potatoes, kale, onion, pepper, garlic, soy milk, parsley and salt.

Turn into the crust and spread evenly.

Dot with butter, if desired, and bake at 350 degrees F for 20 minutes.

MEXICAN HARVEST HUEVOS

Serves 2-4

INGREDIENTS

2	*Harvest Dinner Patties*
1 Small	*Onion, Sliced*
1 Clove	*Garlic, Minced*
6 Medium	*Mushrooms, Chopped*
½ Cup	*Water*
1 Tbsp.	*Tamari*
4	*Eggs*
⅔ Cup	*Water*
⅛ tsp.	*Coriander*
⅛ tsp.	*Oregano*
To Taste	*Sea Salt*
1 Small	*Tomato, Sliced*
½ Cup	*Your Favourite Hot Salsa*

DIRECTIONS

Bake the patties at 350 degrees F for 20 minutes or until browned. Set aside.

Sauté onion, garlic and mushrooms in ½ Cup of water. Add tamari. Boil down most of the liquid.

Beat the eggs with ⅔ Cup of water.

Add the coriander, oregano, salt, and sautéed vegetables to the egg mixture. Mix well.

Putting it together:

Two small casseroles for single servings, or one medium casserole dish may be used.

If you are using two baking dishes, remember to use only half of each layer for each dish.

First spread the hot salsa in the bottom of the baking dish. Next add tomato slices, and then the Harvest Dinner Patties. Pour egg mixture over the top.

Bake at 350 degrees F for 45 minutes or until set to the touch.

Tempeh Main Dishes

Serves 8

SPANISH PAELLA

Very tasty and colourful

INGREDIENTS

Rice:

6 Cups	Water
3 Cups	Brown Rice
1 tsp.	Sea Salt
½ tsp.	Curry Powder
2 tsp.	Turmeric
1 tsp.	Garlic Powder
1 Tbsp.	Basil
250 g	Tempeh
500 g	Tofu

Marinade:

½ Cup	Tamari
½ Cup	Water
¾ Cup	Cider Vinegar
1 Tbsp.	Rosemary

Gazpacho Sauce:

Your favourite Gazpacho soup recipe to make 4 cups with:

1 Inch	Fresh Ginger, Grated
2 Cloves	Garlic, Pressed
To Taste	Tabasco Sauce

Vegetables:

1 Bunch	Broccoli
2 Medium	Carrots
1 Medium	Zucchini
1 Medium	Yellow Crookneck Squash
1	Red Sweet Pepper
1	Green Pepper
¾ Cup	Parsley
3	Scallions
2 Cups	Mushrooms
1 Cup	Snow Peas or Green Beans
½ tsp.	Saffron

DIRECTIONS

Rice:

Bring water to a boil. Add rice and spices. Cover and return to a boil. Reduce heat and simmer for 40 minutes or until rice is tender.

Cut tempeh and tofu into bite size chunks. Marinate in the tamari, water, vinegar and rosemary for 20-30 minutes.

Make your favourite Gazpacho soup recipe and blend in ginger, Tabasco sauce, and garlic.

Sauté the marinated tofu and tempeh over medium heat for 10 minutes, adding marinade as liquid evaporates.

Chop broccoli, julienne carrots, and slice squash diagonally.

Cut peppers into strips. Chop parsley and scallions, slice mushrooms, and cut green beans if being used.

Steam all vegetables except snow peas until crisp tender. If snow peas are used, steam separately for 1 minute.

Combine rice, tofu, tempeh, and the vegetables with saffron in baking dish.

Bake at 350 degrees F for 15 minutes.

Serve with Gazpacho Sauce.

Photo: Spanish Paella

BOMBAY TEMPEH

Serves 5

INGREDIENTS

750 g	Grain Tempeh
1 Tbsp.	Cider Vinegar
1 Tbsp.	Minced Garlic
1 Tbsp.	Minced Fresh Ginger
1 tsp.	Sea Salt
½ tsp.	Cayenne Pepper
½ Cup	Water
¾ lb.	Red Potatoes
1 Medium	Onion
1 Large	Tomato
¼ Cup	Prepared Chili Sauce
1 Tbsp.	Minced Fresh Chives

DIRECTIONS

Cut tempeh into 9 pieces. Arrange in a single layer in a shallow dish. Mix vinegar, garlic, ginger, salt and cayenne in a small bowl. Rub spice mixture into tempeh. Cover and refrigerate for at least 1 hour. (Can be prepared a day ahead.)

Transfer tempeh to heavy large skillet. Add ½ cup water and bring to boil. Reduce heat to medium and simmer for 20 minutes.

Cut potatoes, onion, and tomato into ¼-inch slices.

Pour chili sauce around tempeh. Arrange potato slices over tempeh in single layer. Cover with onion and tomato slices. Cover and cook over medium heat until potatoes are tender, about 20 minutes.

Place tempeh, potato, onion and tomato slices on platter. Cover with sauce and garnish with chives.

Serve with brown rice.

Serves 6-8

Bavarian Potato Tempeh Tart

Ingredients

1 9-inch	Single Pie Crust

Tempeh Filling:

250 g	Grain Tempeh
1 Small	Onion, Minced
1 Cup	Sauerkraut
1 tsp.	Cider Vinegar
1 tsp.	Paprika
¼ Cup.	Tamari
2 tsp.	Lemon Juice

Potato Filling:

5 Medium	Potatoes
1	Eggs
⅔ Cup	Yogurt or
⅓ Cup	Soy Milk
To Taste	Sea Salt
¼ tsp	Nutmeg
Pinch	Allspice
1 Tbsp.	Butter
1 Tbsp.	Dried Parsley
½ tsp.	Paprika

Garnish:

1 Small	Tomato
	Parsley
	Paprika

Directions

Prepare pie crust in a 9-inch pie pan. Cover and refrigerate until needed.

Steam or boil the tempeh for 10 minutes. Drain and dice into small cubes.

Scrub and dice potatoes. Steam until tender.

While potatoes are cooking, sauté together all tempeh filling ingredients, except the sauerkraut, in tamari and small amount of water. Cook until onion is soft and tempeh has browned. Stir in sauerkraut. Cook for 5 more minutes. Mixture should be moist, but not wet. Set aside.

Mash steamed potatoes and add slightly beaten eggs, yogurt or soy milk, salt, nutmeg, allspice, butter, and parsley. Mix well.

To assemble:

Fill the bottom of the pie crust with the tempeh filling. Cover with the potato filling. You may wish to pipe or swirl the potatoes for a fancier looking dish.

Sprinkle with paprika.

Bake at 375 degrees F for 25-30 minutes until golden. Cool slightly to set before serving. Slice in wedges.

Garnish with tomato wedges and parsley.

ORANGE GINGER GLAZED TEMPEH STEAKS

Serves 2

INGREDIENTS

250 g	Grain Tempeh
2 Tbsp.	Oriental Sesame Oil
3 Lg. Cloves	Garlic, Pressed
1 3" Piece	Ginger, Grated
⅓ Cup	Tamari
¼ Cup	Cider Vinegar
1 2" Piece	Cinnamon Stick
¼ Cup	Orange Marmalade
To Taste	Sea Salt
	Cayenne

DIRECTIONS

Steam or boil tempeh for 10 minutes. Drain.

Cut tempeh into thirds, and then cut each third through the thickness once, making 6 pieces.

Place tempeh in a baking dish.

Combine all other ingredients in a saucepan and simmer for 3 minutes, stirring constantly.

Pour over tempeh and bake for 20 minutes at 350 degrees F.

Serve over rice or noodles.

Serves 4-6

PECAN CRUSTED TEMPEH

INGREDIENTS

500 g	Grain Tempeh
1 Tbsp.	Cider Vinegar
¼ Cup	Tamari
1 Cup	Water
1½ Cups	Oat Bran
1½ Cups	Pecans
6	Eggs
1 Cup	Unbleached Flour

Garlic Mayonnaise:

3 Cloves	Garlic
1 Tbsp.	Fresh Grated Ginger
1 Tbsp.	Oriental Sesame Oil
2 Cups	Soy Mayonnaise
1 Small	Bunch Parsley
2	Scallions
1 Large	Tomato

DIRECTIONS

Steam or bake the tempeh for 10 minutes, and cut into 6 peices. Slice through the thickness of each piece. Marinate in vinegar, tamari, and water for 2 hours.

Pulse oat bran and pecans in a food processor or blender until they are finely chopped. Place in a bowl.

Place eggs in a separate bowl and beat well.

Place unbleached flour in a third bowl.

Dip the wet tempeh into the flour; then into the eggs; then into the oat bran/pecan mixture. Make sure all sides are well-coated.

Place onto an oiled baking dish.

Bake at 350 degrees F for 25 minutes.

Garlic Mayonnaise:

Place the garlic, ginger, oriental sesame oil, and mayonnaise in food processor. Blend. Transfer to small bowl.

Chop the parsley and scallions. Remove seeds from tomato, and chop. Add to mayonnaise. Mix well.

Ready to serve over tempeh.

TEMPEH CROQUETTES

Serves 4-6

INGREDIENTS

500 g	Grain Tempeh
250 g	Tofu
½ Medium	Onion
1 Stalk	Celery
2 Cups	Raw Spinach
1 Cup	Grated Carrot
1 tsp.	Marjoram
1 tsp.	Oregano
1 tsp.	Paprika
2 tsp.	Fresh Dill
¼ tsp.	Thyme
¼ tsp.	Cayenne
2 Tbsp.	Tamari
⅓ Cup	Chopped Fresh Parsley
½ Cup	WW Bread Crumbs

Soy Milk Sauce:

4 Tbsp.	Butter or Oil
1 Small	Onion, Chopped
4 Tbsp.	WW Flour
4 Cups	Hot Soy Milk
1 tsp.	Garlic Powder
2 Tbsp.	Tamari

Breading:

1 Cup	Cornmeal
¼ Cup	WW Flour
¼ tsp.	Sea Salt
1 Tbsp.	Paprika

DIRECTIONS

Steam the tempeh for 10 minutes; drain and grate coarsely.

Crumble tofu and mix with tempeh.

Chop finely the onion, celery, and spinach and steam with the grated carrot.

Combine the tofu, tempeh, and, vegetables with herbs, spices, tamari, parsley, and bread crumbs.

Soy Milk Sauce:

Sauté the onion until tender in butter or oil, in a heavy saucepan. Add the flour, stirring constantly a few minutes. Slowly add the hot soy milk while stirring. Add the garlic powder and tamari and cook until smooth and thick. Do not boil.

Add half of this sauce to the tempeh mixture and retain the other half to serve with the croquettes.

Breading:

Mix the cornmeal, flour, salt and paprika in a small shallow bowl.

Form the tempeh mixture into cakes and roll in the breading.

Bake on oiled cookie sheet at 350 degrees F for 1 hour.

Serve with more soy milk sauce or with tartar sauce (see Mock Fish Sticks for recipe).

Makes 4

Tempeh Fajitas

Ingredients

500 g	Grain Tempeh
3 Cloves	Garlic, Minced
4 tsp.	Oregano
1 tsp.	Cumin
2 tsp.	Seasoned Salt
4 Tbsp.	Orange Juice
4 Tbsp.	Vinegar
Dash	Tabasco Sauce
1 Medium	Onion
1 Medium	Green Pepper
1 Medium	Red Sweet Pepper
4	Flour Tortillas
2 Cups	Shredded Lettuce
4	Scallions, Chopped
1½ Cups	Salsa

Directions

Boil or steam the tempeh for 10 minutes. Drain. Cut tempeh into 12 strips.

Combine garlic, seasonings, orange juice, vinegar and Tabasco sauce to make marinade. Add tempeh and marinate for an hour.

Cut onion and peppers into strips.

Sauté tempeh until brown. Add onion and peppers and sauté until tender. Divide among warmed flour tortillas and fold over or roll up.

Pour heated salsa over each tortilla, garnish with lettuce and sprinkle with scallions.

Serve immediately

TEMPEH WITH MUSTARD SAUCE

Serves 6

INGREDIENTS

500 g	Grain Tempeh
1 Tbsp.	Mustard Seeds
Marinade:	
¾ Cup	White Grape Juice
2 Tbsp.	Tamari
¾ Cup	Water
¼ Cup	Dijon Mustard
⅛ tsp.	Cayenne
Sauce:	
2 Cloves	Garlic, Pressed
¼ Cup	Mashed Tofu
1 tsp.	Fresh Rosemary or
½ tsp.	Dried Rosemary
1½ tsp.	Arrowroot or Cornstarch
1 Tbsp.	Cold Water
4	Scallions, Chopped

DIRECTIONS

Slice through the thickness of the tempeh and cut each piece into 6 strips.

Dry roast the mustard seeds in a heavy 9-inch skillet until they pop. Combine these with the marinade ingredients in a casserole dish and add tempeh.

Cover the casserole dish and bake for 30 minutes at 350 degrees F.

Remove baked tempeh from oven. Drain the excess marinade into skillet. Leave the tempeh in the casserole dish and keep warm.

Add garlic, mashed tofu, and rosemary to the marinade in the skillet. Simmer and stir for 5 minutes.

Combine arrowroot or cornstarch with cold water.

Add slowly to sauce while stirring. Simmer and stir until thickened.

Pour sauce over baked tempeh.

Garnish with scallions. Serve immediately.

Serves 6-8

VEGETABLE CRUSTED PIZZA

A hearty and tasty variation on an old favourite

INGREDIENTS

Crust:

4 Medium	Zucchini
3	Eggs, Beaten
⅔ Cup	Unbleached Flour
⅔ Cup	Grated Parmesan Cheese
½ tsp.	Basil

Filling:

250 g	Grain Tempeh, Thawed
1½ tsp.	Chili Powder
1 Tbsp.	Tamari
1	Red Sweet Pepper, Sliced
1	Green Pepper, Sliced
3 Cups	Sliced Mushrooms
1 14-oz. Can	Artichoke Hearts, Drained and Chopped
1 8-oz. Can	Tomato or Pizza Sauce

Optional:

Grated Cheddar Cheese for Garnish

DIRECTIONS

Coarsely grate zucchini. Measure out 8 cups into a bowl. Lightly salt and let sit 10 minutes to sweeten and tenderise. Squeeze out excess juice.

Combine the zucchini with eggs, flour, Parmesan cheese and basil. Press into an oiled 9 x 13-inch baking pan.

Bake crust at 350 degrees F for 30 minutes or until it is set. Brush crust with oil and broil until just golden.

While crust is baking, steam tempeh for 10 minutes. Chop into very small cubes. Combine with chili powder and tamari.

Lightly sauté or steam the peppers and mushrooms.

Spread the sauce on the crust. Layer other ingredients including the artichoke hearts on top. Garnish with grated cheddar cheese, if desired.

Bake at 350 degrees F until heated through and grated cheese, is melted.

Vegetable Tempeh Roast

A simple and healthy meal

Ingredients

250 g	Grain Tempeh
1 Medium	Potato
1 Large	Carrot
1 Medium	Onion
1 Clove	Garlic
2	Bay Leaves
½ Cup	Water or Vegetable Broth
To Taste	Tamari

Directions

Cut the tempeh, potato, and carrots in ½-inch cubes. Slice onion in small wedges. Mince the garlic.

Place bay leaves in the bottom of a small casserole dish. Add tempeh, then carrots, potatoes, onions, and garlic. Pour tamari over tempeh and vegetables. Add water or broth and cover casserole.

Bake at 350 degrees F for 1 hour or until vegetables are tender.

Serves 4

TRUCKERS' DELIGHT

A hearty meal after a good day's work

INGREDIENTS

250 g	Grain Tempeh
½ Cup	Tamari
½ Cup	Water
2⅓ Cup	Soy Milk
1	Bay Leaf
4 Tbsp.	Butter or Light Oil
4 Tbsp.	Unbleached Flour
1 tsp.	Thyme
2	Egg Yolks
1 Cup	Elbow Macaroni
2 Cups	Soy Cheddar Cheese
1 Cup	Soy Parmesan Cheese
½ Cup	Peas
1 14-oz. Can	Tomatoes, Chopped
¾ Cup	WW Bread Crumbs
To Taste	Tabasco Sauce

DIRECTIONS

Marinate tempeh for 1 hour in the tamari and water. Mash and brown in a large frying pan.

Heat the soy milk with bay leaf. Do not boil.

Over medium heat in a heavy saucepan, melt the butter, stir in the flour, and cook a few minutes, but not to brown. Remove from heat, and slowly add the hot milk. Remove the bay leaf and discard. Add thyme and cook a few more minutes.

Remove from heat and add the egg yolks.

Cook the macaroni according to package directions so it is al dente.

In a large bowl, mix together the cooked macaroni, tempeh, sauce, ½ of the Cheddar cheese, most of the Parmesan cheese, the peas, and the chopped tomatoes. Season with Tabasco sauce, if desired.

Pour into a well-oiled baking dish and cover with the remaining Cheddar and Parmesan cheeses.

Top with bread crumbs.

Bake at 350 degrees F without lid for 25-30 minutes.

TARRAGON TOMATO TEMPEH BAKE

Serves 6-8

INGREDIENTS

750 g	*Grain Tempeh*
1 Cup	*Tamari*
½ Cup	*Cider Vinegar*
1 Cup	*Water*
5 Large	*Onions*
½ Cup	*Butter*
2¼ Cups	*Water*
1	*Vegetable Bouillon Cube*
¾ tsp.	*Tarragon*
9 Tbsp.	*Unbleached Flour*
3 Cups	*Crushed Canned Tomatoes*
1 Cup	*Soy Milk, Heated*

DIRECTIONS

Steam or boil the tempeh for 10 minutes. Drain. Cut into strips about 3 inches wide. Then slice each strip through its thickness to make thin pieces.

Combine the tamari, vinegar, and 1 Cup of water. Marinate the tempeh in this mixture for 20 minutes.

Cut the onions into rings no more than ¼-inch thick. Sauté the onions with butter in a large pot until they are translucent. Take care not to burn them.

Boil 2¼ cups of water and add the bouillon cube, stirring to dissolve.

Add the tarragon and flour to the onions and mix well. Then add the tomatoes and broth made from the bouillon cube.

Let this thicken a little; then turn off the heat and stir in the hot soy milk.

Place ⅓ of the sauce on the bottom of a 9-inch square baking dish. Put a layer of grain tempeh on top of the sauce. Continue with another layer of sauce, then tempeh, and end with sauce on the top.

Bake at 350 degrees F for 45 minutes.

Serves 4

SPANISH FILLET OF TEMPEH

INGREDIENTS

500 g	*Grain Tempeh*
Marinade:	
⅓ Cup	*Tamari*
¾ Cup	*Vegetable Stock or Water*
1 Tbsp.	*Olive Oil*
2 Tbsp.	*Cider Vinegar*
1 tsp.	*Basil*
½ tsp.	*Oregano*
¼ tsp.	*Thyme*
½ tsp.	*Rosemary*
1 Tbsp.	*Paprika*
2 Cloves	*Garlic, Crushed*
Dash	*Tabasco Sauce*
Vegetables:	
½ Medium	*Spanish Onion*
1 Medium	*Carrot*
1 Medium	*Bell Pepper*
2 Large	*Tomatoes*
2 Tbsp.	*Fresh Parsley*

DIRECTIONS

Steam or boil tempeh for 10 minutes. Drain. Cut into 8 long strips.

Mix all ingredients for the marinade in a small bowl.

Place strips of tempeh in a baking dish and pour marinade over the top. Chill for about 1 hour.

Bake tempeh in an oven-proof baking dish for 30 minutes at 375 degrees F.

While tempeh is baking prepare the vegetables:

> Cut onion into thin wedges.
> Slice the carrot into thin rounds.
> Cut the bell pepper into strips.
> Cut the tomatoes into wedges.

Steam the vegetables until crisp tender.

Mince the parsley and toss it with all the vegetables in a bowl. Spread them over the tempeh and return to oven for an additional 20 minutes or until the vegetables are roasted to your liking. Serve over a rice pilaf with a green salad.

OUTDOOR BARBECUED TEMPEH

Serves 4 to 6

INGREDIENTS

500 g	Grain Tempeh

Marinade:

⅓ Cup	Oil
1½ tsp.	Paprika
2 tsp.	Onion Powder
½ tsp.	Garlic Powder
1 tsp.	Peanut Butter

Barbecue Sauce

2 Tbsp.	Oil
1 tsp.	Onion Powder
1 Clove	Garlic, Pressed
2 Cups	Tomato Sauce
¼ Cup	Honey
1 Tbsp.	Molasses
2 Tbsp.	Prepared Mustard
½ tsp.	Parsley
¼ tsp.	Sea Salt
¼ tsp.	Allspice
1 Tbsp.	Lemon Juice
1 Tbsp.	Tamari

DIRECTIONS

Blend well all marinade ingredients.

Cut tempeh into 6 pieces, making long rectangles. Place in flat baking dish and cover with marinade. Let sit for 3 to 12 hours.

Place all barbecue sauce ingredients in a medium-sized saucepan. Bring to a boil and immediately reduce to low heat.

Simmer for 20 to 30 minutes. Remove from heat.

Ready briquettes on backyard barbecue.

Remove tempeh from marinade. Add the remaining marinade to the sauce and stir in well.

As you barbecue the tempeh brush generously with sauce, turning several times until well coated and heated through. Should take approximately 10 minutes, depending on how hot your coals are.

Servers 4-5

MOUSSAKA

INGREDIENTS

500 g	Grain Tempeh
2 Tbsp.	Tamari
1 Small	Eggplant
1 Medium	Summer Squash or Zucchini
1 Tbsp.	Butter or Oil
½ Medium	Onion, Chopped
¼ Cup	Raisins (Optional)
1	Tomato, Chopped
¼ Cup	Chopped Parsley
½ tsp.	Cinnamon
¾ tsp.	Nutmeg
¼ tsp.	Cayenne Pepper
½ Cup	Grape Juice
6 Tbsp.	Butter
6 Tbsp.	Unbleached Flour
2 Cups	Soy or Dairy Milk
2	Eggs
½ Cup	Bread Crumbs

DIRECTIONS

Bake tempeh according to directions on the package. Crumble and toss with tamari. Set aside.

Cut peeled eggplant crosswise into ½-inch thick slices and bake on a greased baking sheet at 300 degrees F for 15 minutes.

Cut squash in ¼ to ½-inch rounds and steam for 4 minutes.

Sauté onion in 1 Tbsp. butter, oil or water. Add raisins, tomato, parsley, cinnamon, ½ tsp. nutmeg, cayenne and grape juice and simmer for 20 minutes.

Sauce:

Melt 6 Tbsp. butter in a large pan and whisk in flour. Simmer 1 minute, stirring with a wooden spoon.

Add milk and stir over moderate heat until thick and smooth.

Add 3 Tbsp. of sauce to tempeh mixture.

Beat eggs and ¼ tsp. nutmeg in blender and add a little sauce. Combine egg mixture with sauce in pan and stir until thick.

Sprinkle 9-inch square baking pan with bread crumbs .

Place eggplant in bottom of pan, cover with tempeh mixture, and top with squash. Cover with sauce.

Bake at 350 degrees F for 45 minutes.

INDIAN POTATO & TEMPEH PATTIES WITH TOMATO SAMBAL

Serves 4

Stock your cabinet with Indian Spices and this recipe will mix up easily

INGREDIENTS

250 g	Grain Tempeh
½ Cup	Tamari
1 tsp.	Cider Vinegar
⅛ tsp.	Cumin
⅛ tsp.	Coriander
⅛ tsp.	Garlic Powder
2 Large	Potatoes
¼ Cup	Green Peas
1 tsp.	Nutritional Yeast
3 Drops	Tabasco Sauce
½ tsp.	Sea Salt
½ tsp.	Cumin
½ tsp.	Coriander
½ tsp.	Garlic Powder
¼ Cup	Minced Scallions
2 tsp.	Oriental Sesame Oil (Optional)
1	Egg, Beaten (or Oil)
¾ Cup	WW Bread Crumbs
1 Tbsp.	Dried Parsley
½ tsp.	Turmeric

Sauce for Serving with Patties:

1 tsp.	Grated Fresh Ginger
1 tsp.	Minced Fresh Garlic
¼ Cup	Chopped Scallions
4 Tbsp.	Oil
2 Cups	Tomato Sauce
1 tsp.	Minced Fresh Parsley
½ tsp.	Turmeric
¼ tsp.	Cayenne
1 tsp.	Cumin
1 tsp.	Mustard
½ tsp.	Salt
2 tsp.	Cider Vinegar
To Taste	Tabasco

DIRECTIONS

Boil or steam tempeh for 10 minutes. Drain.

Combine tamari, cider vinegar, and ⅛ tsp. each cumin, coriander, and garlic powder. Marinate tempeh in mixture for 1 hour.

Cube potatoes and steam until tender.

Steam peas.

Mash potatoes with nutritional yeast, 3 drops Tabasco sauce, and ½ tsp. each salt, cumin, coriander, and garlic powder.

Fold peas and scallions into the potatoes.

Remove tempeh from the marinade. Mash the tempeh or grind in food processor and then sauté well in oil. Add to potato mixture.

Taste and add sesame oil, if desired.

Form into 5 patties.

Dip into egg (or oil), then into bread crumbs which have been mixed with parsley and turmeric.

Bake in a well-oiled shallow pan without lid for 1 hour at 375 degrees F.

Sauce:

Sauté ginger, garlic and scallions in oil for a few minutes. Add tomato sauce, parsley, and spices. Cook over low heat for 5 minutes. Add vinegar and Tabasco sauce to taste. Serve over baked patties.

Serves 4

HOT & COLD SESAME NOODLES

INGREDIENTS

10 oz.	Flat Noodles
3 Tbsp.	Oriental Sesame Oil
½ Cup	Tahini
¼-½ Cup	Water
1 Tbsp.	Chili Oil
2 Cloves	Garlic, Crushed
3 Tbsp.	Red Wine Vinegar
¼ Cup	Tamari
4	Scallions, Chopped
1 Tbsp.	Chopped Parsley
250 g	Grain Tempeh or Tofu

DIRECTIONS

Cook noodles according to package directions. Rinse and cool. Toss with 1 Tbsp. sesame oil. Set aside.

Mix tahini with water until smooth. Stir in remaining sesame oil, chili oil, garlic, vinegar, and tamari.

If using tempeh, steam for 10 minutes. Allow to cool. Chop or shred tempeh or tofu.

Pour sauce over noodles and toss with scallions, parsley and tofu or tempeh.

CHINESE BARBECUE TEMPEH VEGETABLES

Serves 3

INGREDIENTS

250 g	Grain Tempeh

Marinade:

¾ Cup	Cider Vinegar
¼ Cup	Tamari
¼ Cup	Water
¼ Cup	Honey
1 tsp.	Mustard Powder
1 tsp.	Freshly Grated Ginger Root

Sauce:

3-4 Cloves	Garlic, Pressed
½ Cup	Pineapple Juice
3 Tbsp.	Cornstarch

Vegetables:

½ Cup	Carrots, Sliced
½ Medium	Zucchini, Sliced
½ Cup	Mushrooms, Sliced
½ Cup	Broccoli Florets
½ Cup	Snow Peas
	Bok Choy or Cabbage, Chopped, or Mung Bean Sprouts
	Cooked Brown Rice

DIRECTIONS

Boil or steam tempeh for 10 minutes. Drain and slice in thin strips. Mix marinade ingredients in blender and pour over tempeh. Marinate overnight, if possible, or 1-2 hours.

Cook garlic in pineapple juice for 5 -10 minutes. Remove tempeh from marinade and set aside. Use some of the marinade to dissolve the cornstarch. Add cornstarch mixture and rest of the marinade to the pineapple juice. Stir until thickened. More cornstarch may be needed depending on desired thickness. Once thickened, add the tempeh strips.

Steam vegetables, except the mung been sprouts, until crisp tender. Add mung beans sprouts.

Serve over brown rice.

Optional:

Marinated tempeh strips may be cooked on a grill after marinated.

Serves 6-8

TEMPEH & BROCCOLI IN SPICY CASHEW SAUCE

INGREDIENTS

500 g	Grain Tempeh
1 Cup	Cashews
2	Onions
2 Bunches	Broccoli
½ Cup	Vegetable Oil
¼ Cup	Water
¼ Cup	Tamari
2 Tbsp.	Cornstarch
2 Tbsp.	Cider Vinegar
⅔ Cup	Water
¼ tsp.	Cayenne
To Taste	Sea Salt
2 Cups	Water
	Cooked Brown Rice

DIRECTIONS

Steam the tempeh for 10 minutes. Cut into ½-inch cubes.

Toast the cashews lightly.

Cut the onions into halves lengthwise and slice them thin crosswise. Cut the broccoli into florets and small chunks.

Whisk together 1 Tbsp. of the oil, ¼ cup of water, tarmari and cornstarch until the cornstarch is dissolved. Add the tempeh and stir until it is evenly coated. Let marinate 8-24 hours.

Drain and save the marinade.

In a blender, finely grind ½ of the cashews with 4 Tbsp. of oil, the vinegar, ⅔ cup of water, the cayenne and salt.

In a large skillet heat 3 Tbsp. of oil over moderate heat and sauté the tempeh until golden. Transfer it with a slotted spoon into a large serving dish.

Then sauté the onions until golden. Add the broccoli, the reserved marinade, and 2 cups water and cook covered for 3 minutes or until the broccoli is just tender.

Stir in the cashew sauce and the tempeh.

Place in serving dish on brown rice and sprinkle with remaining cashews.

Tempeh Parmesan

Serves 6-8

Ingredients

750 g	Grain Tempeh
½ Cup	Tamari
½ Cup	Water
4 Tbsp.	Vinegar
Sauce:	
½	Onion, Chopped
½	Green Pepper, Chopped
2 Cloves	Garlic, Minced
1 Tbsp.	Butter or Light Oil
3 Cups	Tomato Sauce
½ tsp.	Basil
½ tsp.	Oregano
1	Egg
1 Tbsp.	Water
⅔ Cup	Bread Crumbs
1 Cup	Parmesan Cheese
To Taste	Garlic Powder
To Taste	Sea Salt
1 lb.	Spinach
1 Cup	Mozzarella Cheese
1 Cup	Cheddar Cheese
Pinch	Dried Parsley

Directions

Boil or steam tempeh for 10 minutes. Drain. Cut tempeh into bars 2 inches wide. Slice through thickness of each bar. Marinate in the tamari, vinegar and ½ cup water for no less than 30 minutes. While tempeh marinates, make the sauce.

Sauce:

Lightly sauté the onion, green pepper, and garlic in butter or oil. Add tomato sauce, basil and oregano. Simmer for 20 minutes.

Beat the egg with 1 Tbsp. of water. In a separate bowl, mix the bread crumbs, Parmesan cheese, garlic powder and salt. Reserve a little of the Parmesan cheese for the topping.

Dip marinated tempeh in egg, then dredge lightly in bread crumb mixture. Brown tempeh on each side in a lightly oiled skillet.

Wash spinach in hot water, just to soften. Shake off excess water .

Preheat oven to 375 degrees F.

In baking dish layer:

⅓ of sauce
½ of tempeh
mozzarrella (reserve a little for the topping)
spinach
⅓ of sauce
rest of the tempeh
rest of the sauce

Top with Cheddar cheese, the reserved mozzarella and Parmesan. Add a pinch of dried parsley for colour. Bake for 30-45 minutes.

Tofu Main Dishes

TOFU CACCIATORE

Makes 2 Cups

INGREDIENTS

1 kg	Tofu
Marinade:	
3 Cups	Water
1	Carrot, Chopped
1 Stalk	Celery, Choped
½	Onion, Chopped
1 Sprig	Fresh Parsley Minced
¼ tsp.	Cayenne
½ tsp.	Oregano
½ tsp.	Basil
1-2	Bay Leaves
½ tsp.	Ground Celery Seed
2 Cloves	Garlic, Pressed
Pinch	Thyme
Pinch	Savoury
Pinch	Marjoram
3 Tbsp.	Olive Oil
3 oz.	Red Grape Juice
3 oz.	Tamari
½ Cup	WW Flour
½ Cup	Durum Flour
2 Medium	Onions
1 lb.	Mushrooms
1 16-oz. Can	Whole Canned Tomatoes
1 8-oz. Can	Tomato Sauce
3 Tbsp.	Olive Oil
1 tsp.	Sea Salt
2 oz.	Tomato Paste

DIRECTIONS

Freeze the tofu overnight. Thaw (you may boil in hot water to thaw in a hurry), and squeeze out water. Cut into large bite-size cubes. Set aside.

Bring the water for the marinade to a boil, adding the carrot, celery, onion, and parsley. Boil for 20 minutes.

In the last 5 minutes, add all the spices except the salt. Remove from heat and strain out vegetables.

Take 2 cups of the stock and add the olive oil, tamari and grape juice to it. Chill. When cool, marinate the tofu for 15 to 20 minutes, making sure the tofu is well covered with liquid. Remove the tofu from the marinade and squeeze some of the liquid out.

Combine the two flours and toss the tofu in it until well coated.

Brush a skillet with oil and sauté the tofu until it is golden brown on all sides. Remove from the skillet and set aside.

Cut the onions coarsely. Quarter the mushrooms and tomatoes.

Sauté the onions in the olive oil until translucent.

Add the tomatoes with their liquid , the tomato sauce, mushrooms, and the remains of the marinade (liquid and vegetables).

Bring to a boil and add the tofu and salt. Cook for 10-15 minutes stiring gently. Add tomato paste. Cook for another 3 minutes.

Serve over linguini noodles.

Makes 5-6 burgers

VEGETARIAN TOFU BURGERS

INGREDIENTS

⅓ Cup	Minced Carrot
⅓ Small	Onion, Minced
⅓ Cup	Chopped Parsley
750 g	Tofu
2 tsp.	Dry Mustard
½ tsp.	Garlic Powder
⅛ tsp.	Thyme
½ tsp.	Chili Powder
1 Tbsp.	Tamari
2 Tbsp.	Tahini
1 Tbsp.	Lemon Juice
3 Tbsp.	Catsup
Optional:	
2	Eggs, Slightly Beaten
¼ Cup	Oat Bran or Ground Quick Cooking Oat Flakes

DIRECTIONS

In a food processor, mince the carrot, onion and parsley. Place them in a large bowl.

Finely crumble 500 g of tofu into the same bowl.

Break up the remaining tofu into food processor, add the seasonings, tamari, tahini, lemon juice, and catsup. Blend until smooth.

Add this mixture to the chopped vegetables and crumbled tofu. Mix well. Add eggs,if using, and form into 5-6 round patties. (If the mixture is too wet to form into patties, mix in oat bran or ground oats flakes.)

Cook in a very lightly oiled frying pan at medium heat, until golden on both sides. Serve on a toasted whole-wheat bun or your favourite bread. Top the burger with "Tofu Thousand Island Dressing".

This recipe also makes a good stuffing for manicotti shells or filling for lasagna.

Serves 8-10

TOFU & TEMPEH GOULASH

A most requested dish at The Vegetarian Restaurant. Don't let the list of ingredients scare you. Start cooking!

INGREDIENTS

4 Tbsp.	Paprika
2 Tbsp.	Chili Powder
2 Tbsp.	Basil
2 Tbsp.	Oregano
1 Tbsp.	Thyme
1 tsp.	Caraway Seeds
1½ Tbsp.	Garlic Powder
⅛ tsp.	Allspice
Pinch	Poultry Seasoning
½ Cup	Tamari
1 Cup	Grape Juice
1 Cup	Vegetable Stock or Water
¼ Cup	Cider Vinegar
500 g	Grain Tempeh
375 g	Tofu
4 Cups	Sliced Mushrooms
2 Small	Onions, Sliced
1 Clove	Garlic, Minced
2 Stalks	Celery, Chopped
1 Cup	Sliced Cabbage
1 Medium	Carrot, Sliced
2 Medium	Bell Peppers Cut into Strips
1 Medium	Zucchini, Sliced
1 28-oz. Can	Whole Tomatoes, Chopped
⅔ Cup	Sauerkraut
½ Cup	Chopped Parsley
½ Cup	Chopped Fresh Dill
1 Cup	Sour Cream
To Taste	Tabasco Sauce

DIRECTIONS

In a small bowl, combine all spices down to and including the poultry seasoning.

In another container, combine tamari, grape juice, vegetable stock and vinegar.

Cut tempeh and tofu into small cubes and place in a shallow baking pan.

Sprinkle with half of the spice mixture and half of the liquid mixture. Toss to coat thoroughly.

Bake at 375 degrees F for 45 minutes.

In a large pot, combine mushrooms, onions, garlic, celery, cabbage and carrot. Add the remaining spice mixture and liquid. Bring to a boil, then reduce heat and simmer for 10 minutes.

Add peppers and zucchini. Cook another 5 minutes.

Add tomatoes, sauerkraut, parsley, dill, sour cream, and Tabasco sauce and continue to cook to heat through.

Serve with brown rice or egg noodles tossed with poppy seeds and parsley.

Serves 6

TOFU & VEGETABLES IN SZECHUAN BLACK BEAN SAUCE

INGREDIENTS

500 g	*Firm Tofu*
8 Cups	*Mixed Vegetables: Carrots, Broccoli, Celery, Mushrooms, Cauliflower, Zucchini, Onions, Bok Choy*
¼ Cup	*Tamari*
1 Clove	*Garlic*
2 Tbsp.	*Chinese Preserved Black Beans*
½ Inch	*Fresh Ginger Root, Grated*
1 Cup	*Vegetable Stock*
1 Tbsp.	*Mild Honey*
½ tsp.	*Cider Vinegar*
2 Tbsp.	*Cornstarch or Arrowroot*
2 Tbsp.	*Cold Water*
1 Tbsp.	*Oriental Sesame Oil*
4 Shakes	*Tabasco Sauce*

DIRECTIONS

Cut tofu into 1-inch cubes.

Cut vegetables thinly with an Oriental flair. Cut carrots, celery, zucchini on the diagonal.

Combine the tofu, vegetables, tamari, garlic, preserved black beans, ginger, vegetable stock, honey and vinegar in a heavy saucepan.

Ingredients should be at room temperature for speedy heating. Bring ingredients to a boil and simmer until vegetables are more crisp than tender.

Mix the arrowroot or cornstarch in 2 tablespoons of water. Return the sauce to a boil and add the starch mixture, stirring well until you have a glazed texture. Add the sesame oil and Tabasco. Remove from heat. Adjust tamari to taste.

Serve over brown rice or noodles.

Serves 4

TOFU À LA QUEEN

INGREDIENTS

375 g	Tofu
1 Small	Carrot
1 Small	Onion
½ Cup	Chopped Mushrooms
½ Cup	Peas
3 Tbsp.	Butter
3 Tbsp.	Unbleached Flour
2 Cups	Hot Soy Milk
1 tsp.	Prepared Mustard
To Taste	Tamari
¾ tsp.	Sea Salt
½ tsp.	Poultry Seasoning
½ tsp.	Paprika

Biscuits:

1¼ Cup	Unbleached Flour, Sifted
½ Cup	Soft WW Flour
½ tsp.	Sea Salt
1 Tbsp.	Double Acting Baking Powder
6 Tbsp.	Butter
1 Cup	Soy Milk

DIRECTIONS

Cut the tofu into ½-inch cubes. Sauté for 5 minutes in tamari and water. Drain.

Dice the carrot, chop the onion and mushrooms, and steam with the peas until tender.

Melt the butter in a small heavy saucepan on low heat. Add the flour and stir one minute. Slowly add the hot soy milk.

Add the seasonings, except paprika, and simmer and stir over low heat until thickened.

Combine the tofu, vegetables and sauce and pour into a 2-quart casserole. Sprinkle with paprika. Bake for 20 minutes at 350 degrees F.

Serve over soy milk biscuits.

Biscuits:

Sift together the flours, salt, and baking powder. Put in food processor with butter and pulse for a few seconds until mixture is crumbly. Turn out into a medium bowl and add the soy milk.

Stir until the mixture is uniformly moist.

Drop by the spoonful onto an ungreased baking sheet.

Bake at 450 degrees F for 12 to 15 minutes until golden brown.

TOFU STUFFED ACORN SQUASH

Serves 6

INGREDIENTS

2 Tbsp.	Butter or Sunflower Oil
¾ Cup	Chopped Onion
1 Cup	Chopped Celery
½ Cup	Chopped Mushrooms
250 g.	Tofu, Drained & Mashed
1 Medium	Carrot, Grated
1 Large	Apple, Grated
2	Eggs, Beaten
1 tsp.	Sea Salt
½ tsp.	Sage
¼ tsp.	Cayenne
½ tsp.	Poultry Seasoning
10-12	Slices of WW Bread, Cubed
3	Acorn Squash

DIRECTIONS

Sauté onion, celery, mushrooms and tofu in butter or oil until the onion is tender but not browned.

Remove from heat and combine with carrot, apple, eggs and seasonings. Mix well.

Mix in bread cubes.

Cut the squash into halves and remove the seeds. Score the squash halves and put a pat of butter in each, if desired.

Fill each half with stuffing.

Place in an oven-proof baking dish with 1 inch of water in the bottom.

Bake, covered, at 350 degrees F for 1 hour or until the squash is tender.

Top the your favourite gravy and serve.

Serves 6

Tofu Broccoli Quiche

Ingredients

1 9-inch	Single Pie Crust
4	Eggs
375 g	Tofu
⅓ Cup	Soy or Dairy Milk
Pinch	Nutmeg
To Taste	Sea Salt
1 tsp.	Basil
¼ Cup	Soy Mayonnaise
1 Bunch	Broccoli
1	Onion

Directions

Prepare pastry and line a 9-inch pie plate.

Whisk or blend together in a food processor eggs, tofu, milk, nutmeg, salt, basil and mayonnaise (regular mayonnaise may be used).

Wash and chop the broccoli into medium chunks. Chop the onion.

Steam the broccoli and onion just until tender. Place in bottom of pastry-lined pie plate.

Pour liquid mixture over vegetables. Bake for approximately 35 minutes at 350 degrees F or until center of quiche is set.

TOFU MANICOTTI

Serves 6

INGREDIENTS

14	Manicotti Shells
1 kg	Tofu, Crumbled
1 Medium	Onion, Chopped
2 Cloves	Garlic, Minced
1 Tbsp.	Minced Parsley
1½ Quarts	Tomato Sauce

DIRECTIONS

Cook manicotti shells in boiling (salted) water according to instructions on package. Drain and allow to cool.

Mix tofu, onion, garlic and parsley. Stuff each shell with this mixture.

Pour ½ of the tomato sauce in the bottom of a baking dish. Place stuffed shells on top. Pour remaining sauce over the manicotti.

Cover and bake 40 minutes at 350 degrees F or until piping hot.

The recipe for Vegetarian Tofu Burger also makes a good dairy-free stuffing for manicotti shells as well as a filling for lasagna.

Serves 4

TOFU VEGGIE SOUFFLÉ

INGREDIENTS

1 Small	Onion, Chopped
1 Tbsp.	Butter
½ Cup	Niblets Corn
1 Cup	Finely Chopped Asparagus
1½ Cups	Chopped, Stewed Tomatoes
½ tsp.	Oregano
½ tsp.	Basil
3 Cloves	Garlic, Minced
3	Eggs, Beaten
250 g	Tofu, Mashed
1 Tbsp.	Sunflower Oil
1½ Tbsp.	Lemon Juice
½ tsp.	Sea Salt

DIRECTIONS

Sauté onion in butter until soft.

Place in 1½-quart casserole.

Add corn, asparagus, tomatoes, oregano and basil.

Place remaining ingredients in a blender and blend until smooth.

Add to casserole and bake at 350 degrees F for 45-60 minutes or until firm.

SWEET & SOUR TOFU VEGETABLES

Serves 4-6

INGREDIENTS

½ Medium	Red Sweet Pepper, Sliced
½ Medium	Green Pepper, Sliced
½ Medium	Yellow Pepper, Sliced
1 Large	Onion, Sliced
1½ Cups	Julienne Carrots
1½ Cups	Diagonally Cut Celery
1½ Cups	Florets of Broccoli
1½ Cups	Sliced Mushrooms
500 g	Tofu, Cut into ¾-inch Cubes
	Tamari

Sauce:

2 Cloves	Garlic, Pressed
2 Tbsp.	Fresh Grated Ginger
¼ Cup	Tamari
1 Cup	Water
4 Cups	Pineapple Juice
2 Tbsp.	Tamari
¼ Cup	Cider Vinegar
4 Cloves	Garlic
⅛ tsp.	Powdered Ginger
⅓ Cup	Oriental Sesame Oil
3½ Tbsp.	Arrowroot or Cornstarch
¼ Cup	Cold Water

DIRECTIONS

Steam all of the vegetables just until tender.

Sprinkle the tofu with tamari and bake on an oiled cookie sheet for 15 minutes at 350 degrees F.

Sauce:

Simmer 2 cloves garlic and ginger in ¼ Cup tamari and 1 Cup water for 5-10 minutes.

Blend the pineapple juice, 2 Tbsp. tamari, vinegar, 4 cloves garlic, powdered ginger, and sesame oil. Add to above.

Make a paste of the arrowroot or cornstarch and cold water. Whisk it into the simmering sauce. Continue cooking a few minutes until thickened.

Serve tofu-vegetable mixture on a bed of egg noodles or brown rice.

STUFFED TOFU

Serves 6

INGREDIENTS

750 g	Tofu
½ Cup	Tamari
1½ Cup	Water
1½ Cup	Cider Vinegar
4 Cloves	Garlic
4 Cups	Mushrooms
1 Head	Celery
	Water or Broth
1 Tbsp.	Rosemary
1 Tbsp.	Basil
2 tsp.	Oregano
¼ tsp.	Celery Salt
	Pinch Poultry Seasoning
	Bread Crumbs

DIRECTIONS

Slice tofu into ¼-inch slices. Marinate in tamari, water and vinegar for 20 minutes. Drain. Then sauté over medium heat, 5 minutes on each side until golden.

Slice half of the garlic, mushrooms, and celery. Chop the other half.

Sauté all the vegetables in a small amount of water or broth until tender. Add seasonings.

Then add enough bread crumbs to vegetables so that the mixture is firm, but moist.

Lay half of the tofu in a large baking dish. Cover each slice of tofu with stuffing and top each piece with another slice of tofu.

Bake for 15 minutes at 350 degrees F.

Serve with your favourite gravy.

Oriental Tofu

Serves 2-4

Ingredients

2 Tbsp.	Oil
2 Cloves	Garlic, Minced
1	Onion, Sliced
2 1" Pieces	Ginger Root or
¼ tsp.	Ground Ginger
500 g	Tofu, Cubed
To Taste	Tamari
1 Tbsp.	Molasses
Optional:	
	Mung Bean Sprouts
	Mushrooms
	Celery
	Bok Choy
	Broccoli
	Cauliflower

Directions

Brown garlic and onion in oil in a heated skillet or wok.

Add all the other ingredients except the molasses. Mix well. Simmer 3-5 minutes.

Stir in molasses just before removing from heat.

Any sliced vegetables of your choice (e.g., sliced mushrooms, celery, bok choy, broccoli, cauliflower) can be added to the onions.

Mung bean sprouts can be added in with the molasses so they stay crisp.

Serves 4

BAVARIAN NOODLES

INGREDIENTS

6 oz.	Egg or Other Wide Noodles
8 Cups	Water
½ Cup	Chopped Onions
1 Tbsp.	Sunflower Oil or
2 Tbsp.	Water
500 g	Tofu, Crumbled
2 Cups	Soy or Dairy Sour Cream
1 Tbsp.	Poppy Seeds
½ tsp.	Sea Salt
2 Cups	Cooked Peas
½ tsp.	Sea Salt
3 Tbsp.	Soy or Dairy Parmesan Cheese
Optional:	
	Cayenne Pepper

DIRECTIONS

Cook the noodles in 8 Cups of water and drain.

Sauté onions in oil or water.

Add crumbled tofu, sour cream, poppy seeds and salt to sautéed onions.

Mix peas in drained noodles and add sour cream mixture. Turn into a 1½-quart oiled baking dish.

Sprinkle with the soy Parmesan cheese and place in oven.

Bake at 350 degrees F for 25 minutes or until heated through.

Optional:

Sprinkle with cayenne.

VEGETABLE NUT CROQUETTES

Serves 6

A Vegan Recipe

INGREDIENTS

4 Cups	Mushrooms, Chopped
2 Medium	Onions, Chopped
4 Cloves	Garlic, Crushed
¼ Cup	Water
5 Medium	Carrots, Grated
2 Cups	Almonds, Ground
1 Cup	Soymash
250 g	Firm Tofu, Crumbled
250 g	Firm Tofu, Blended
2 tsp.	Nutritional Yeast
2½ tsp.	Basil
¼ tsp.	Thyme
¾ tsp.	Oregano
½ tsp.	Garlic Powder
½ tsp.	Poultry Seasoning
1 tsp.	Sea Salt
⅛ tsp.	Allspice
2 Tbsp.	Parsley, Minced
½ tsp.	Mustard Powder
Pinch	Nutmeg
Optional:	
	Sesame Seeds

DIRECTIONS

Cook the mushrooms, onions, and garlic in the water over medium heat for 15 minutes. Remove from heat. Drain.

Grate the carrots and steam slightly. Set aside.

Purée the mushrooms, onions, garlic and carrots in a food processor.

In a large mixing bowl combine the almonds, soymash, tofu, yeast, herbs and spices.

Add puréed vegetables and mix thoroughly.

Oil a large cookie sheet. Using your hands or a small ice cream scoop, form the mixture into balls.

Place on cookie sheet and bake at 350 degrees F for 30 minutes until golden brown.

Serve with your favourite mushroom gravy or a herbed tomato sauce.

Optional:

Sprinkle with sesame seeds before baking.

Other Main Dishes

Serves 6

CURRIED NOODLE CASSEROLE

INGREDIENTS

½ lb.	Wide Egg Noodles
2 Medium	Onions
2 Medium	Tomatoes
¼ Cup	Butter or Light Oil
¼ Cup	Water
1 tsp.	Mustard Seeds
¼ tsp.	Coriander
1 Tbsp.	Curry Powder
¼ tsp.	Tamari
4 Cloves	Garlic
12	Falafels

Curry Sauce:

1 Tbsp.	Light Oil or Butter
½ Cup	Unbleached Flour
2 Cups	Soy or Dairy Milk, Scalded
1 Tbsp.	Curry Powder
1 tsp.	Sea Salt
1 Tbsp.	Tamari
¾ lb.	Mushrooms
1 Cup	Chopped Red Sweet Pepper
1 Cup	Chopped Broccoli
1 Cup	Chopped Carrot
½ Cup	Chopped Squash
½ Cup	Peas

Optional:

Toasted Cashews

Chutney

DIRECTIONS

Cook, drain, and set aside noodles.

Dice the onions and tomatoes and sauté in butter or oil and water, along with the mustard seeds, coriander, curry powder and ¼ tsp. tamari.

Crush the garlic and add, along with crumbled falafels. Simmer for 5 minutes and remove from heat. Set aside.

To make the sauce, melt the butter or oil in a heavy saucepan. Add the flour, stirring over minimum heat for a few minutes. Slowly add the hot milk, stirring constantly. Add the curry powder, salt, and 1 Tbsp. tamari. Continue cooking and stirring until smooth and thickened.

Steam the vegetables for 5 minutes.

In a large bowl, mix together the thickened curry sauce and the steamed vegetables.

In a large baking dish, first place the falafel and tomato mixture, then the noodles, and lastly the curry sauce-vegetable mixture.

Bake at 350 degrees F for 40 minutes.

May be garnished with toasted cashews and served with chutney.

SOYMASH ONION ENCHILADAS

Serves 6

INGREDIENTS

12	Corn Tortillas
Salsa:	
2 Cups	Onions, Finely Chopped
4 Cloves	Garlic, Crushed
4 Tbsp.	Olive Oil
½ tsp.	Cayenne
2 tsp.	Chili Powder
2 tsp.	Salt
3 tsp.	Cumin
6 Cups	Chopped Tomatoes
2 Cups	Water
½ tsp.	Cider Vinegar
4 Tbsp.	Tomato Paste
To Taste	Tabasco Sauce
Filling:	
4 Medium	Onions
2 Cloves	Garlic
1	Jalapeño Pepper
1 Medium	Green/Red Pepper
1½ tsp.	Sea Salt
¼ Cup	Water or
1 Tbsp.	Butter or Oil
2½ Cups	Soymash
2½ Cups	Grated Cheese (Monterey Jack or Mild Cheddar)
1 tsp.	Cumin
2 tsp.	Chili Powder

DIRECTIONS

Salsa:

In a large sauce pan, sauté onions and garlic in olive oil, until the onions are translucent. Add the spices and cook 1 minute longer. Add the remaining ingredients and simmer for aproximately 20 minutes.

Filling:

Mince or pulse in a food processor the onions, garlic, jalapeño pepper, and the green pepper.

Sauté above vegetables in a large pot at medium heat with ¼ cup of water or 1 Tbsp. of butter or oil.

Cover and let simmer for 10 minutes.

Stir in soymash, 1½ Cups grated cheese and spices.

Set filling aside.

To prepare tortillas, coat a frying pan in oil. Working quickly when pan is hot, fry each side of tortilla for 30 seconds and set aside.

Spread a thick layer of the filling on each tortilla. Then roll the tortilla, folding the ends in as you roll.

Cover the bottom of a baking dish with a layer of salsa. Place the tortilla rolls in the dish and cover with the salsa. Sprinkle 1 Cup grated cheese on top.

Bake at 350 degrees F for ½ hour.

MOCK FISH STICKS

Serves 4-6

INGREDIENTS

Sticks:

1 19-oz. Can	Chick Peas, Drained
1 14-oz. Can	Artichoke Hearts
1 Medium	Onion
2 Stalks	Celery
2 Cloves	Garlic
¼ Cup	Olive Oil
2 Tbsp.	Lemon Juice
1 tsp.	Celery Seed
½ Cup	Catsup
¼ Cup	Prepared Mustard
1	Egg, Beaten
250 g	Tofu
1 Cup	Oat Bran
1 Cup	Soymash
	Sunflower Oil orButter

Tartar Sauce:

2 Cups	Soy Mayonnaise
1 Tbsp.	Prepared Mustard
½ Cup	Catsup
3	Pickles, Diced Fine
1 Tbsp.	Horseradish, Grated or Prepared

DIRECTIONS

Sticks:

Put chick peas, artichoke hearts, onion, celery and garlic into food processor. Using the steel blade, pulse to mince ingredients. Transfer to medium-sized bowl and add olive oil, lemon juice, celery seed, catsup and mustard.

Blend egg with tofu and add to above mixture.

Have 1 cup oat bran and 1 cup soymash measured out in separate cups. Add ¾ of the soymash and ½ of the oat bran to the chick pea mixture.

Form into fish stick-shaped patties. If mixture is not stiff enough, add more soymash and oat bran until easily formed.

Brush lightly with oil or butter.

Bake 30-40 minutes at 350 degrees F.

Serve with tartar sauce.

Tartar Sauce:

Mix all ingredients together.

Breakfast & Brunch

Serves 6-8

TEXAS CORN CAKE

A hearty fill-you-up food with a touch of Mexican heat

INGREDIENTS

6	Harvest Dinner Patties
1 Cup	WW Flour
1 tsp.	Sea Salt
4 tsp.	Double Acting Baking Powder
2½ Cups	Cornmeal
3	Eggs
1 Small	Onion
3-6	Green Chilli Peppers (May be canned)
2 Cups	Soy or Dairy Milk
½ Cup	Oil
½ Cup	Honey
1 12-oz. Can	Niblets Corn, Drained
	Your Favourite Salsa

DIRECTIONS

Lightly brown Harvest Dinner Patties in 350 degree F oven. Crumble into an oiled 9 x 13-inch baking dish. Set aside.

Sift together the whole-wheat flour, baking powder and the salt. Add the cornmeal and mix.

Beat the eggs in a separate bowl.

Grate the onion, mince the peppers, and add them to the eggs.

Add the soy milk, oil, honey and corn to the egg mixture.

Combine all ingredients with a few quick strokes. Pour the batter over the crumbled patties.

Bake at 350 degrees F for 35-40 minutes until corn cake tests done.

Serve with tomato salsa.

Photo: For breakfast or brunch. Clockwise from top right, Texas Corn Cake, Harvest Patty Breakfast, Soy Milk Waffles, Frothy Carob Cashew Milk, centre, Potato Pancakes.

Serves 4

HARVEST PATTY BREAKFAST

Old MacDonald now has a soybean farm!

INGREDIENTS

4	*Harvest Dinner Patties*
2	*English Muffins*
4	*Eggs*
Optional:	
	Butter for Muffins
	Grated Cheese
	Gravy Packet from Harvest Patty Box

DIRECTIONS

Cook Harvest Dinner Patties according to directions on the box.

While patties are cooking, make the gravy if you are going to use it.

Cook eggs, any style.

Toast English Muffins after slicing into halves. Butter, if desired.

Top each Muffin with one patty and one egg.

Optional:

Top with cheese and warm in toaster oven or under broiler until cheese melts and/or serve with gravy.

Makes 12

POTATO PANCAKES

INGREDIENTS

3 Cups	Grated Raw Potatoes
2	Eggs, Beaten
1 tsp.	Sea Salt
250 g	Tofu, Mashed
1 Small	Onion, Grated
¼ Cup	Any Flour
Optional:	
	Apple Sauce
	Sour Cream

DIRECTIONS

Do not grate potatoes until you are ready to make the batter, as potatoes will discolour soon after grating.

Combine all ingredients in a mixing bowl and mix well.

Fry pancakes in a little oil on medium to medium-high heat until browned on both sides.

Alternatively, bake on a greased baking sheet at 375 degrees F, turning once so that both sides become golden.

Optional:

Serve with apple sauce and/or sour cream.

Makes 8 oz.

HOT & FROTHY CAROB CASHEW MILK

Remember that warm feeling you had when Mom gave you hot milk? Well, here it is again.

INGREDIENTS

2 tsp.	Finely Ground Cashews
8 oz.	Soy Milk
2 Tbsp.	Carob Powder
1 tsp.	Vanilla
2 Tbsp.	Honey
1 Tbsp.	Light Oil
½ tsp.	Molasses

DIRECTIONS

Use blender or coffee grinder to grind cashews very fine.

Heat soy milk but not to boiling.

Place all ingredients into a blender. Blend until smooth and frothy.

Serve immediately.

This drink is also good served cold.

Serves 1

HARVEST DINNER WESTERN OMELETTE

This recipe can be adapted for as many people as you wish to serve

INGREDIENTS

1	Harvest Dinner Patty
3	Eggs
¼ Medium	Green Pepper
½ Small	Onion
	Butter or Oil or Water
Optional:	
	Grated Soy or Dairy Cheese
	Tomato-Style French Dressing

DIRECTIONS

Brown the Harvest Dinner Patty in a skillet large enough to hold the final omelette.

While patty is browning, wash and chop the vegetables.

Remove the Harvest Dinner Patty and set aside.

Steam or sauté the green pepper and onion in the skillet.

Scramble the eggs in a separate bowl. Eggs are best if allowed to warm to room temperature before cooking and cooked over a medium-low heat. This prevents them from becoming tough.

Remove the vegetables from the skillet and wipe skillet clean with a paper towel.

Oil the skillet and begin cooking the eggs.

When the eggs have cooked a few minutes, crumble the Harvest Dinner Patty into them and add the vegetables. Continue cooking until the eggs are done to the desired consistency. If using cheese, sprinkle over eggs. Fold over. Slip onto plate and garnish.

Optional:

Serve with French dressing as a topping.

BLINTZES FOR BRUNCH

Serves 6

INGREDIENTS

3	Eggs
1 Cup	Unbleached Flour
1½ Cups	Water
2 Tbsp.	Sunflower Oil
Filling:	
250 g	Tofu
250 g	Cottage Cheese
¾ tsp.	Cinnamon
½ Cup	Raisins
1 tsp.	Vanilla
1 tsp.	Grated Orange Rind
2	Egg Yolks, Beaten

DIRECTIONS

Place eggs, flour, water and oil in a blender. Blend until well mixed.

Pour into a bowl, cover with a damp cloth or wax paper, and refrigerate for 1 hour and 30 minutes.

Heat a 6-inch crepe pan until hot. Wipe the pan with butter and pour in ¼ cup of the batter. Tilt and rotate the pan so that the batter covers the bottom and sides in a thin layer. Cook on one side only until lightly browned.

Turn out onto paper towels or tea towels.

Makes about 13 crepes.

Filling:

Drain and crumble the tofu.

Mix all of the ingredients together.

Fill the middle of the cooked side of the crepes with 1½ Tbsp. of the tofu mixture. Fold the flaps in to form a square shape.

Place folded ends down on a lightly oiled baking sheet.

Bake at 400 degrees F until browned.

Dot each crepe with butter and sprinkle with cinnamon.

Makes 6-8

SOY MILK WAFFLES & PANCAKES

INGREDIENTS

Dry Mix to be Stored and Used as Needed:

Dry Ingredients:

4 Cups	Soft WW Flour
4 Tbsp.	Baking Powder
1 tsp.	Sea Salt

Wet Ingredients (For 1 Cup of Dry Mix):

2	Eggs
¾ Cup	Soy Milk
½ Cup	Melted Butter or Oil

DIRECTIONS

Sift all dry ingredients together and store in airtight container in your refrigerator or freezer.

To make 6 to 8 waffles:

Use 1 cup dry mix (at room temperature is best).

Combine wet ingredients and whisk well.

Add the cup of dry mix. Whisk only until it is all wet. Some lumps may still be visible.

Cook according to directions given with your waffle iron.

May also be used for pancakes.

Desserts

Serves 6

BLACK BOTTOM PIE

This recipe makes an exceptionally delicious pie

INGREDIENTS

1 9-inch	Single Pie Crust
1½ tsp.	Agar-agar
¾ Cup	Water
Bottom Layer:	
¼ Cup	Melted Butter
3 Tbsp.	Carob Powder
3 Tbsp.	Water
250 g	Tofu
⅓ Cup	Honey
1 tsp.	Tahini
1 tsp.	Vanilla
1 tsp.	Cinnamon
2 tsp.	Peanut Butter
Pinch	Sea Salt
Middle Layer:	
250 g	Tofu
⅓ Cup	Honey
2 tsp.	Tahini
1½ tsp.	Vanilla
1½ tsp.	Cinnamon
Pinch	Sea Salt
Top Layer:	
125 g	Tofu
2 Tbsp.	Honey
2 tsp.	Vanilla
Pinch	Sea Salt
½ tsp.	Lemon Juice
2 Tbsp	Sunflower Oil
2 Tbsp.	Water or Soy Milk

DIRECTIONS

Prepare your favourite pastry shell and prebake.

Dissolve the agar-agar in ¾ cup water and bring to a boil. Lower heat and simmer for 2 minutes, stirring constantly. Remove from heat, but cover to keep warm so that the agar-agar will not set.

Melt the butter.

Bottom Layer:

Place all of the ingredients for the bottom layer in food processor. Blend until smooth and creamy. Add ½ of the melted butter and ½ of the agar-agar mixture and blend again. Pour into the crust and smooth out.

Middle Layer:

Place all of the ingredients for the middle layer into food processor or blender. Blend until smooth and creamy. Add the rest of agar-agar mixture and melted butter. Blend a few minutes more. Pour over bottom layer and smooth out.

Top Layer:

Clean out food processor or blender, for this last filling is white and will look best if its colour is not darkened by the previous ingredients.

Place all the ingredients for the top layer in the food processor or blender. Blend until very creamy. Pour over the top of the pie and smooth out.

Garnish with nuts or carob chips.

Enjoy!

TOASTED ALMOND TOFU PIE

Serves 6

This pie gets rave reviews from people who are tofu dessert connoisseurs

INGREDIENTS

Garnish:	Nuts or Carob Chips
Crust:	
1½ Cups	Whole Almonds
2 Cups	Oat Flour or Ground Quick-Cooking Oat Flakes
¼ tsp.	Sea Salt
½ Cup	Water
½ Cup	Sunflower Oil
Filling:	
750 g	Tofu
½ Cup	Sunflower Oil
½ Cup	Light Honey
1 Tbsp.	Vanilla Extract
2½ tsp.	Almond Extract
0-¼ Cup	Water

DIRECTIONS

Crust:

Lightly toast almonds. Set aside ½ Cup for garnishing the finished pie. Grind ½ Cup of the almonds in a food processor with the oat flour or ground oat flakes and salt until the nuts are finely ground.

Add ½ cup of water and the oil to the almonds in the food processor. Blend for a few moments. Transfer the mixture into a bowl and let it sit a few moments until it becomes less sticky.

Oil a pie plate and press in the crust making a fluted edge all around. Prick the crust bottom with a fork. Bake at 400 degrees F until golden, about 20 minutes. Crust must be completely cooled before filling is added.

Filling:

Blend the tofu in a food processor until the large lumps disappear. Add all of the other ingredients except the water and process until very smooth and creamy. Test for consistency and taste. You may want to add some water, keeping in mind that the filling does set in time.

Turn into the cooled pie shell. Decorate with sliced or whole toasted almonds. Refrigerate for 1 hour before serving.

Alternative:

Use filling as a pudding or in a parfait, layering with other flavours of tofu pudding. Carob and banana puddings work well.

TOFU PUMPKIN PIE

This pie is dairy-free and egg-free

Serves 6

INGREDIENTS

1 9-inch	Single Pie Crust
250 g	Tofu
2 Cups	Pumpkin Purée
1½ tsp.	Cinnamon
½ tsp.	Cardamon
½ tsp.	Ginger
½ tsp.	Nutmeg
1 tsp.	Sea Salt
1 tsp.	Molasses
⅓ Cup	Sunflower Oil
½ Cup	Honey

Optional:

Additional Honey for a Sweeter Pie

DIRECTIONS

Prepare your favourite pastry for a single crust 9-inch pie. Line the pie pan with the crust.

Blend all ingredients in a food processor until very smooth.

Pour the filling into pie shell.

Bake at 350 degrees F for 45 minutes to 1 hour, or until the center is set.

Cool before slicing.

Optional:

Serve with vanilla soy ice cream.

Serves 6

TOFU CHEESECAKE NUMBER 1

INGREDIENTS

1 9-inch	Graham Cracker Crust
Filling:	
½ Cup	Maple Syrup
3 Tbsp.	Tahini
500 g	Tofu
1 tsp.	Vanilla
2 Tbsp.	Lemon Juice
Pinch	Sea Salt
Pinch	Cinnamon
Topping:	
1 Cup	Strawberries, Raspberries, Cherries or Blueberries
2 Tbsp.	Maple Syrup
¼ tsp.	Cinnamon
½ Cup +2 Tbsp.	Apple Juice
2 tsp.	Arrowroot Powder

DIRECTIONS

Filling:

Blend all filling ingredients in a food processor or blender. Pour into your favourite graham cracker crust.

Bake 15-25 minutes at 350 degrees F or until filling has set. Let cool while making the topping.

Topping:

Combine berries, maple syrup, cinnamon and ½ cup apple juice in a sauce pan.

Dissolve arrowroot in 2 Tbsp. apple juice and stir into fruit mixture. Simmer until thickened and clear.

Let cool and pour over pie.

Serve chilled.

TOFU CHEESECAKE NUMBER 2

Serves 6

INGREDIENTS

1 9-inch	Single Pie Crust
Filling:	
1 Cup	Cashew Meal
¾ Cup	Dates
1 Cup	Water
1 Tbsp.	Vanilla
Juice of	½ Lemon
1½ Tbsp.	Grated Lemon Peel
250 g	Tofu
⅛ tsp.	Cinnamon
¼ Cup	Agar-agar Flakes
½ Cup	Water
Topping:	
1 10-oz. Jar	All Fruit Preserves (no sugar)

DIRECTIONS

Prepare your favourite pie crust and bake until golden. Chill.

Filling:

Prepare cashew meal by grinding cashews in a coffee grinder or food processor. Blend with dates and 1 cup water in food processor until creamy.

Add the next 5 ingredients to the food processor.

In a saucepan combine agar-*agar* flakes and ½ cup water. Boil until flakes dissolve. Add to mixture in the food processor and blend until smooth.

Pour mixture into cooled baked pie shell. Set aside in refrigerator to chill.

Topping:

Melt preserves in a small saucepan over low heat. Spread on cheesecake and chill.

CAROB TOFU FREEZER PIE

Serves 6

INGREDIENTS

Crust:

¾ Cup	Unbleached White Flour
3 Tbsp.	Demerara Sugar
⅓ Cup	Butter
⅓ Cup	Pecans, Chopped

Filling:

¾ Cup	Sweetened Carob Chips
125 g	Tofu, Finely Mashed or Dairy Cream Cheese
2 Tbsp.	Soy or Dairy Milk
⅛ tsp.	Sea Salt
1 Cup	Whipping Cream or Tofu Whipped Cream

Optional:

For Mocha Filling Add:

2 Tbsp.	Coffee Substitute Dissolved in 2 Tbsp. of Hot Water

DIRECTIONS

Crust:

Combine sifted flour and sugar.

Cut butter into flour mixture until it resembles a coarse meal.

Mix in pecans.

Press crust into bottom of a 9-inch pie pan and bake at 375 degrees F for 8 minutes. Cool.

Filling:

Melt carob chips in the top of a double boiler over simmering water. Cool.

Combine remaining ingredients and fold into the chips.

Pour into pie shell and place in freezer.

Chill well. May partially freeze before serving.

Freezes well for future use.

Makes 12

BANANA SOYMASH MUFFINS

INGREDIENTS

½ Cup	Light Oil
1 Cup	Honey
2	Eggs, Separated
1 Large	Ripe Banana, Mashed
½ Cup	Soy Milk
¾ Cup	Soymash
1 tsp.	Liquid Lecithin
½ tsp.	Banana Extract
1½ tsp.	Double Acting Baking Powder
2 Cups	WW Pastry Flour
½ tsp.	Sea Salt

DIRECTIONS

Cream oil and honey together with beaten egg yolks.

Add banana, soy milk, soymash, lecithin, and extract to the above ingredients and mix.

Sift dry ingredients together, then mix with wet ingredients, blending only until all ingredients are wet. Do not overmix.

Beat egg whites until they form peaks. Fold into mix.

Fill oiled muffin tin, or a muffin tin lined with papers.

Bake at 350 degrees F for 25-30 minutes.

Makes 30 cookies

CARROT OATMEAL CHEWS

Moist and slightly chewy. A healthy Vegan snack

INGREDIENTS

1 Cup	Grated Carrots
½ Cup	Light Oil
½ Cup	Demerara Sugar
1 Cup	Soymash
1 tsp.	Vanilla
1 Cup	Coconut
¼ Cup	Flour of Any Kind
1 Cup	Quick-Cooking Oat Flakes
½ tsp.	Sea Salt

DIRECTIONS

Lightly pack the grated carrots into a 1-cup measure and fill with water to 1-cup line.

In a medium-sized bowl, mix the carrots and water, oil, sugar, soymash and vanilla.

Add the coconut, flour, oat flakes and salt. Mix.

Let stand 5 minutes to absorb moisture.

Drop by tablespoons onto an oiled cookie sheet.

Bake for 20-25 minutes at 375 degrees F.

MAPLE PECAN BARS

These bars are a rich dessert and wonderful for special occasions, as they can easily be decorated to be quite beautiful

INGREDIENTS

¼ Cup	Butter, Softened
1 Tbsp.	Light Oil
1¼ Cup	Maple Syrup
1 tsp.	Vanilla
¼ tsp.	Cinnamon
2 Cups	WW Pastry Flour
1 tsp.	Double Acting Baking Powder
1 Cup + ⅓ Cup	Finely Chopped Pecans
500 g	Tofu, Pressed
1 Cup	Plain Yogurt
¼ Cup	Sunflower Oil

DIRECTIONS

Preheat oven to 350 degrees F and oil a 9-inch square pan.

Cream butter, oil, ½ cup maple syrup, ½ tsp. vanilla and cinnamon.

Gradually add flour, baking powder, and 1 cup pecans.

Press evenly into baking pan and bake 20 minutes.

Remove from oven and cool while preparing topping.

To press tofu, place in a shallow bowl and cover with a small dish. Place a 2-3 pound weight, such as a capped jar of water, on top of the dish. This weight will force the excess moisture out of the tofu.

Blend tofu, yogurt, remaining maple syrup and vanilla in a food processor until smooth, about 3 minutes. Add oil and blend for one minute. Spread topping over crust. Sprinkle with ⅓ cup pecans.

Bake an additional 30 minutes.

Remove from oven. Chill slightly before cutting into bars.

Makes 24 cookies

TOFU FUDGE COOKIES

INGREDIENTS

250 g	Tofu
½ Cup	Oil
1½ Cup	Demerara Sugar
½ Cup	Carob Powder
1 Tbsp.	Vanilla
1 Tbsp.	Water, Milk, or Soy Milk
3 Cups	Unbleached Flour
1 tsp.	Baking Soda
1 tsp.	Salt
½ Cup	Chopped Pecans or Walnuts

DIRECTIONS

Blend tofu and oil in food processor until smooth.

Add sugar, carob powder, vanilla and liquid. Mix well.

Sift together flour, baking soda and salt.

Add the flour mixture to the tofu mixture.

Dough will be fairly stiff.

Mix in nuts.

Roll into balls and place on lightly greased cookie sheet.

Bake 12-15 minutes at 350 degrees F.

Makes 24 cookies

MAPLE OATMEAL COOKIES

INGREDIENTS

3 Cups	Quick-Cooking Oat Flakes
1 Cup	Oat Bran
1 Cup	Soymash
1 Cup	Oat Flour
1 Cup	Durum Flour
2 Cups	Raisins
2 tsp.	Cinnamon
2 tsp.	Cardamon
4 tsp.	Double Acting Baking Powder
1 tsp.	Sea Salt
1 Cup	Light Oil
1½ Cups	Maple Syrup
1½ tsp.	Vanilla
½ Cup	Water

DIRECTIONS

Stir together all dry ingredients including the raisins.

Whisk together all wet ingredients.

Combine wet and dry ingredients. Batter should be moist. If batter seems dry, add a bit of water.

Form batter into firm balls using a scant ⅓ cup batter for each cookie, or use a spring-loaded ice cream scoop to measure out the cookies. Space the balls about 2 inches apart on an oiled cookie sheet.

Flatten cookies to ½ inch thick. Cookies will be very large.

Bake at 350 degrees F for 25 minutes or until slightly browned.

Makes about 24 very large cookies.

Makes 40-50 cookies

SOYMASH MACAROONS

INGREDIENTS

1 lb.	Butter, Softened
2 Cups	Honey
4	Eggs, Beaten
2 Cups	Soymash
1 Tbsp.	Vanilla
¼ - ½ tsp.	Almond Oil or Extract
½ tsp.	Sea Salt
4 Cups	Durum Flour
3 Cups	Coconut

DIRECTIONS

Cream softened butter with honey. Add beaten eggs, soymash, vanilla, almond oil or extract, salt, durum flour and coconut.

Can be rolled into small balls and slightly flattened with a fork for baking or can be rolled into a log, wrapped in wax paper and chilled to slice later for baking.

Bake on an ungreased baking sheet at 350 degrees F for 20 to 25 minutes.

Serves 4

Carob Mocha Tofu Pudding

Ingredients

750 g	Tofu
½ Cup	Sunflower Oil
¾ Cup	Honey
⅓ Cup	Carob Powder
2½ Tbsp.	Instant Coffee or Coffee Substitute
½ tsp.	Sea Salt
½ tsp.	Cinnamon
½ tsp.	Vanilla

Directions

Place all ingredients in a food processor and blend until tofu becomes very smooth.

Serve chilled.

Alternative:

You can use this as a pie filling in your favourite baked crust.

RASPBERRY TOFU PARFAIT OR PIE

Serves 6-8

INGREDIENTS

2 Cups	*Fresh Raspberries*
750 g	*Tofu*
½ Cup	*Light Honey*
¼ tsp.	*Vanilla*
½ Cup	*Sunflower Oil*
½ Cup	*Lemon Juice*
1 tsp.	*Agar-agar*
2 Tbsp.	*Water*
Optional:	
	Fresh Mint Leaves

DIRECTIONS

Set aside ½ Cup of the raspberries to place on top of the finished parfaits.

Place the tofu, honey, vanilla, oil and lemon juice in a food processor. Blend until smooth. Leave the mixture in the food processor.

Place 1½ Cups raspberries, the agar-agar, and the water in a small pot and bring to a boil over medium heat. Cook for 2 minutes, stirring constantly. Remove from heat.

Turn on the food processor and slowly add the raspberry mixture. Blend until smooth.

Fill individual parfait glasses and top with raspberries which you have set aside.

Garnish with fresh mint leaves.

Alternatives:

Make up a recipe of tofu topping from the Black Bottom Pie recipe. Use this to make coloured layers in your parfait glasses.

If making a pie, fill a 9-inch baked pie shell with the raspberry filling and top with the topping from the Black Bottom Pie recipe. Then decorate with the reserved raspberries.

Serves 6

CREAMY CAROB TOFU PUDDING

INGREDIENTS

½ Cup	*Dates*
⅓ Cup	*Cashews*
¾ Cup	*Apple Juice*
½ Cup	*Sunflower Oil*
500 g	*Tofu*
3 Tbsp.	*Vanilla*
⅓ Cup	*Carob Powder*
1 tsp.	*Lemon Juice*

DIRECTIONS

Chop the dates.

Place the dates and cashews in a blender or food processor with the apple juice. Blend or process for a few moments.

Add remaining ingredients and blend well.

Best if refrigerated overnight before serving.

Photo: Desserts, clockwise beginning at the top, Tofu Parfaits, Cheesecake No. 1, Black Bottom Pie, Maple Pecan Bars, Soymash Macaroons, Carrot Oatmeal Chews, Banana Soymash Muffins

Makes 24

BANANA DATE CHEWS

INGREDIENTS

3	*Ripe Bananas*
1 Cup	*Finely Chopped Dates*
½ Cup	*Sunflower Oil*
1 tsp.	*Vanilla*
1 Cup	*Soymash*
1 Cup	*Quick-Cooking Oat Flakes*
½ tsp.	*Sea Salt*
½ Cup	*Chopped Pecans*

DIRECTIONS

Put into blender or food processor the bananas, dates, oil and vanilla. Blend for 1 minute.

Turn into a bowl and stir in the soymash, oat flakes, salt and pecans.

Let stand for 5 minutes to absorb moisture.

Drop by tablespoon onto an ungreased cookie sheet.

Bake at 350 degrees F for 20-25 minutes.

Holiday Recipes

Serves 5

FRENCH CANADIAN TOURTIERE

A light protein version of the traditional Christmas and New Year's Pie

INGREDIENTS

125 g	Frozen Tofu
⅛ - ¼ Cup	Tamari
Pastry:	
3 Tbsp.	Unsalted Butter
2 Tbsp.	Sunflower Oil
½ tsp.	Liquid Lecithin
1¾ Cups	Pastry Flour
¼-½ tsp.	Sea Salt
1 Tbsp.	Lemon Juice
3 Tbsp.	Cold Water
Filling:	
2¾ Cups	Water
2	Bay Leaves
¾ Cup	Brown Lentils
1 Clove	Garlic, Pressed
1 Medium	Onion, Finely Chopped
1 Cup	Finely Chopped Mushrooms
1 Medium	Potato
2 Cups	Soymash
⅛ tsp.	Ground Cloves
¼ tsp.	Ground Cinnamon
⅛ tsp.	Ground Sage
⅛ tsp.	Savoury
Pinch	Nutmeg
1 Tbsp.	Olive Oil

DIRECTIONS

Thaw tofu, squeeze out water and dice very fine. Marinate in the tamari.

Pastry:

Cut the butter into pieces. Combine with oil and lecithin. Cut this mixture into flour and sea salt until it resembles a coarse meal. Mix lemon juice and cold water and blend lightly into flour mixture until you can gather dough into a ball. Wrap and refrigerate for 20 minutes or place in freezer for 10 minutes. Divide dough into 2 pieces. Roll out one piece for bottom crust and line a 9-inch pie plate.

Filling:

Bring water to a boil. Add bay leaves, lentils, marinated tofu, garlic, onion, and mushrooms. Cover and simmer for 15 minutes. Check to see if the lentils are tender.

Grate the potato and add to mixture. Cook for an additional 15 minutes.

Add the soymash, spices and olive oil. Stir well and cook a few minutes until heated through. Remove bay leaves. Fill pie shell and cover with top pastry. Cut air vents in top crust and crimp edges to seal.

Bake in preheated 400 degree F oven for 10 minutes. Reduce heat to 350 degrees and bake for 30 minutes or until golden brown.

Let the pie set for 20 minutes before serving.

Serve with cranberry sauce.

Serves 4

HARVEST PATTIES EN CROUTE

Relatively easy to prepare, but rich and tasty, this dish has an impressive presentation

INGREDIENTS

4	Harvest Dinner Patties

Crust:

3⅓ Cups	Unbleached Flour
¼ tsp.	Sea Salt
1 Cup	Butter
⅔ Cup	Yogurt
2 tsp.	Fresh Lemon Juice
2	Eggs, Beaten

Filling:

1 Large	Potato
1¼ Cups	Finely Cubed Vegetables: Bell Pepper, Potato, Carrot, Summer Squash, Onion, Corn, Peas
1 Tbsp.	Butter
1 tsp.	Vegetable Seasoning
2 Tbsp.	Chopped Parsley

Egg Wash:

	1 Egg Yolk &
	2 Tbs. Soy Milk

DIRECTIONS

Bake Harvest Dinner Patties in 350 degree F oven for 15 minutes. Set aside to cool.

Crust:

Sift together the flour and salt. Cut in the butter with a pastry blender.

Combine the yogurt, eggs and lemon juice. Mix this with the flour to form a soft dough. Chill for 30 minutes.

Filling:

Steam the potatoes and mash with butter and, if desired, salt.

Steam the finely cubed vegetables with the peas and/or corn until just tender. In a bowl mix the vegetables with vegetable seasoning, the mashed potatoes, and the parsley.

Assembling:

Roll out ½ of the pastry on a lightly floured board to ⅛ inch thickness. Cut out 4 pastry pieces the shape of the Harvest Patty, but adding a 3-inch border on all sides.

Place patties on a lightly oiled baking sheet. Divide the vegetable filling among the patties, pressing slightly so that the filling matches the shape of the patty. Drape the pastry pieces over the patties, tucking any excess under the patties. Make a small slash in the top of the pastry to allow steam to escape.

Brush pastry with egg wash.

Bake in an oiled pan at 375 degrees F for 35-45 minutes or until golden. Serve with gravy.

Makes 1 Quart

HOLIDAY SEASON SOY NOG

Rich and cheery, a delight to share with friends on cold winter nights

INGREDIENTS

3 Cups	Unflavoured Soy Milk
3 Tbsp.	Honey
3 Tbsp.	Sunflower Oil
1½ tsp.	Natural Rum Extract
2 tsp.	Natural Vanilla
1 tsp.	Grated Nutmeg

DIRECTIONS

Place all ingredients in a blender. Blend until smooth and frothy.

Store in glass container in refrigerator.

Very nice served warm, but be careful not to overheat as soy milk will curdle at high heat.

Photo: Holiday Dishes. Clockwise from bottom right. Holiday Nut Loaf, Holiday Season Soy Nog, Tofu Roulade, Soy Milk Custard, Harvest Dinner en Croût;, centre, French Canadian Tourtière.

Soy City Foods Vegetarian Cookbook

TOFU ROULADE

Serves 6

A simple recipe, yet an elegant centerpiece for a very special meal

INGREDIENTS

1 lb. Large	Mushrooms, Sliced
½ Cup	Onions, Chopped
2 Tbsp.	Sunflower Oil or Water
750 g	Tofu, Crumbled
¼ Cup	Nutritional Yeast
⅓ Cup	Tamari
½ Cup	Chopped Parsley
Pinch	Basil
Pinch	Thyme
Pinch	Cayenne Pepper
Dough:	
2 Cups	Unbleached Flour
½ Cup	Soft WW Flour
Pinch	Sea Salt
⅓ Cup	Sunflower Oil
⅔ Cup+3 Tbsp.	Cold Water

DIRECTIONS

Filling:

Lightly sauté mushrooms and onions in oil or water. In a bowl, combine with the rest of the filling ingredients and mix well. Set aside.

Dough:

In a medium-sized bowl, combine the whole-wheat and unbleached flours with the salt. Mix in the oil. Then add the cold water and form into a ball.

Roll dough out on a floured surface to approximately 10 x 12 inches.

Spread the filling evenly over the entire dough area leaving a 1-inch margin on all sides.

Fold over one 10-inch end and begin rolling until all is rolled. Moisten closing flap with a bit of water to seal. Pinch the ends closed.

Gently prick the top several times with a fork.

Bake at 400 degrees F for 25 minutes or until golden brown.

Serves 5-6

SOY MILK CUSTARD

Light and delicious, a fine dessert after a holiday meal

INGREDIENTS

4	Eggs
¼ tsp.	Cinnamon
⅓ Cup	Honey
¼ tsp.	Nutmeg
½ tsp.	Sea Salt
1 tsp.	Vanilla
2½ Cups	Soy Milk
Garnish:	
	Pistachio Nuts
	Fresh Pomegranate Seeds

DIRECTIONS

Beat eggs with a whisk while slowly adding other ingredients. If using a blender or mixer, all ingredients can be put in at once.

Pour into 6 oven-proof custard cups.

Place cups into a deep baking pan and fill the pan with water to ⅔ of the level of the custard.

Bake at 350 degrees F for 60-70 minutes .

When you remove the pan from the oven, remove the cups from the pan or they will continue to cook.

Serve warm or cold.

Cool to room temperature before refrigerating.

Garnish:

For the holidays, try garnishing this custard, after it has cooled, with pistachio nuts and fresh pomegranate seeds.

HOLIDAY NUT LOAF

Serves 6

INGREDIENTS

½ Cup	Ground Pecans or Brazil Nuts or Combination
¼ Cup	Ground Cashews
¼ Cup	Ground Almonds
250 g	Tofu
3	Eggs, Beaten
1 Medium	Onion, Minced
1 Tbsp.	Tamari
1½ Tbsp.	Catsup
1 tsp.	Garlic Powder
¾ tsp.	Poultry Seasoning
½ Cup	Wheat Germ
¼ Cup	Oat Bran
¼ Cup	Engevita Yeast

DIRECTIONS

When measuring ground nuts pack the cup firmly.

Tofu should be well drained and dried in a tea towel.

Using a grinder or food processor, grind the nuts as finely as possible. If using a food processor, add the tofu and blend well. Then do the rest of the mixing by hand.

If using hand method for the nuts and tofu, cream them together in a large bowl using the back of a large spoon.

Add the beaten eggs, minced onion, tamari, catsup, garlic powder and poultry seasoning. Mix well. Add the wheat germ, oat bran and yeast. Mix well.

Turn into a glass loaf pan which has been lightly coated with a combination of oil and liquid lecithin. This will help the loaf to turn out of the pan nicely for a better presentation.

Cover the pan with foil and bake at 350 degrees F for 30 minutes.

Remove the foil and continue baking for another 30 minutes or until the loaf has browned .

Let sit 10 minutes.

Turn onto platter and garnish with parsley and vegetables.

Serve with mushroom or cashew gravy.

GLOSSARY

Agar-agar

This is a sea vegetable used as a substitute for gelatin in cooking; it is rich in vitamins B, C, D, and A, Calcium, Iron, and Phosphorous. It will set at room temperature in about 30 minutes or can be chilled to speed the process. It is available in most health and natural food stores.

Apple Cider Vinegar

This vinegar is the recommended alternative to common, distilled vinegar for its purity. It is high in potassium and malic acid, the latter being an aid to digestion.

Arrowroot

This is a nutritious thickening agent made from a tropical American plant. It can be processed without the addition of chemicals. It is used in a manner similar to cornstarch.

Bamboo Shoots

These somewhat acidic Oriental plants complement many foods well. They come packed in cans and usually can be found in regular supermarkets.

Black Beans, Dried and Preserved

This is a very flavourful ingredient. Made from black soybeans, they are fermented in water with salt, ginger, orange peel, with various spices added. Common to Oriental food stores, they are often called "Fermented Black Beans" or "Preserved Black Beans".

Black Chinese Mushrooms, Dried

These come in different varieties with names like "Cloud ears" or "Wood ears". An edible food commonly found in Chinese cooking, they provide both taste and texture. It is generally recommended that they be soaked overnight or 15-20 minutes in warm water before using. Their stems are tough and should be trimmed.

Bok Choy

A Chinese vegetable of the cabbage family, it has thick white stalks with dark green leaves. The entire vegetable can be cooked.

Bouillon Cubes, Vegetable or Soy Based

As their names suggest, these helpful ingredients can be made from soy or vegetables and are used to make stock or liquid bases. Usually containing various spices, they can also be salty.

Bulgur

This is cracked whole-wheat grain, either parboiled or dried, which can vary in quality from coarse to fine.

Carob Powder

Naturally sweet and made from a bean with a flavour resembling that of chocolate, it is a good alternative to the latter. Unlike chocolate it has no caffeine and a texture much like cocoa.

Cayenne

Made from a variety of the pepper plant in the Capsicum family, it is not only used in this book, but recommended as a condiment preferable to black pepper. There is a growing body of evidence which shows that although both produce "heat" within the body, black pepper does it by irritation of the digestive system, and cayenne does it by stimulation. Cayenne has been found to be a stimulant to the metabolism in general.

Chicken-Flavoured Seasoning

A vegetable-based bouillon that is seasoned to taste much like chicken.

Engevita Yeast

This is a type of nutritional yeast (see Nutritional Yeast).

Extract

This is a preparation containing the essence of a substance — such as vanilla, almond, or peppermint — in concentrated form. Natural extracts avoid artificial ingredients and tend to be stronger.

Flours

Many different flours are available as alternatives to common white flour. For example: Whole-wheat pastry flour, while it acts much like an unbleached white pastry flour, is a ground, whole-grain, soft wheat and is nutritionally superior to the latter. Whole-wheat flour is ground from a hard, red, winter wheat. High in protein, it is a versatile ingredient in any kind of baked goods.

Miso

This is a fermented soybean paste, very high in protein and vitamin B-12. Originally from Japan, it is a salty seasoning that goes well in soups. A common item in any health or natural food store, it can be stored in the refrigerator (once opened) in a tightly closed container for many months.

Molasses

Rich in minerals, particularly iron, this sweetener improves the lasting qualities of many baked goods. Molasses is a by-product of sugar production, the most nutritious type being blackstrap molasses.

Mung Bean Sprouts

These sprouts are best eaten raw or lightly cooked. They are easily grown from tiny green mung beans which are available in most health food stores. The sprouts also can be purchased at many supermarkets and certain health food stores. They have a high protein content and are more digestible raw than when cooked.

Noodles (or Pasta)

There are many types of noodles available which can not only add shape, colour, and texture to a meal but also health. Food sources range from Durum Semolina and Semolina enriched with egg to Whole Wheat, Quinoa (an ancient South American grain which leads the pack in protein) or Spelt (another ancient grain high in protein, carbohydrates and fiber), and Jerusalem Artichoke, Rice, Spinach or Mung Bean.

Nori

This sea vegetable is the richest one in protein. Also high in vitamins B, C, and A as well as calcium, magnesium, and phosphorous, this nutritious food comes cholesterol-free in green, purplish or olive brown sheets. Available at health or natural food stores.

Nutritional Yeast

These yellow, powdery flakes are high in B-Vitamins. They are less bitter and more pleasant than brewer's yeast.

Oils

Much can be said regarding the processed oils found in most supermarkets as opposed to what are often called "cold-pressed" oils. In truth, the latter is a contradictory term because both so-called "cold-pressed" and regularly processed oils are heated to some extent. The real difference is what happens after that initial heating. Most commercial brands get degummed, refined, bleached and deodorized. Their vitamin E content, which has been shown to protect the body's highly unsaturated fatty acids from damage, is removed along with other vital substances. Also, commercial processing often involves heating the oil to 250 degrees C and it results in an unnatural and hydrogenated product. The bottom line when buying oils is to check whether the item is unrefined and mechanically (such as expeller) pressed. Chemical treatments in the place of mechanical pressing make either fatty or trans-fatty acids that are definitely not "helpful" to the body.

Oriental Sesame Oil or Dark Sesame Oil

This is a fragrant product of roasted sesame seeds. It is popular in East Asia to flavour foods. Light sesame oil, which is made from raw sesame seeds, is more common in western countries. The dark oil can be found in most Oriental or health food stores and is used more as a flavouring than for cooking.

Peanut Butter

There are better alternatives to the average commercial brands of peanut butter. By shopping in a health or natural food store, one can usually avoid all the artificial colours, flavours, sweeteners, or preservatives common to most popular brands sold in supermarkets.

Pita Bread

This is a "flat" or "pocket" bread made in Middle-Eastern bakeries. It is round and usually made from white or whole-wheat flour without yeast.

Sea Salt

This salt is commonly both sun and kiln-dried. It is better than common table salt because it contains a high level of many naturally occurring trace minerals.

Soymash

Also called Okara, it is the fibrous part of soybeans which remains after the soybeans have been cooked and pressed to remove the soymilk. If soymash is unavailable, moistened oat bran may be substituted in recipes.

Soy Milk

This nutritious alternative to dairy milk comes from pressing ground, cooked soybeans. Its protein content is higher than regular cow's milk, and although lower in calcium it has several outstanding qualities: its level of iron is higher, it has no cholesterol, virtually no sodium, and is low in fat. It will keep about seven days in the refrigerator and for people allergic to dairy milk it is a good alternative. Look for it in health food stores, tofu shops, or Oriental markets.

Tahini

Of Middle Eastern origin, it is made from ground sesame seeds. It has a creamy texture and a rich, nutty flavour and is high in both protein and calories.

Tamari

This is an aged, fermented soy sauce made from soy beans, salt, and water. (Some types do contain wheat.) It is darker in colour and richer and stronger in flavour than commercial soy sauce and usually is made without any sort of added colour, sweeteners or preservative.

Index